A Book Girl's Guide
to Marietta

A Book Girl's Guide to Marietta

TULE
PUBLISHING

Table of Contents

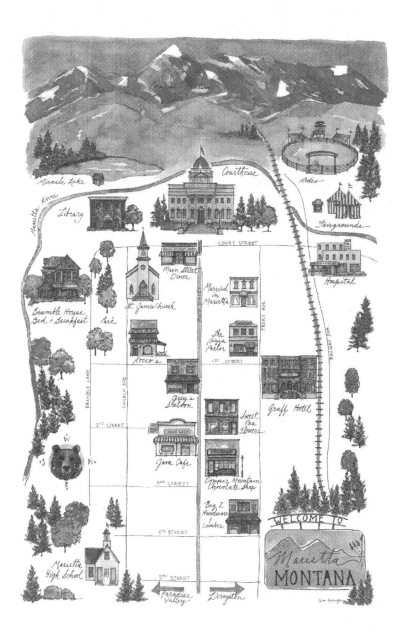

FOREWORD

CJ Carmichael

Creating a fictional town is one of the joys of being an author and the fun is magnified when the creative process involves a team of highly imaginative and talented writers. When Jane Porter, Megan Crane, Lilian Darcy and I sat around the kitchen table at my cottage on Flathead Lake, Montana, in May of 2013 our goal was to invent a locale for the connected rodeo stories we planned to write.

We drew maps, we hammered out details, and we researched real Montana towns and history to make our town feel as authentic as possible. Important town landmarks were fabricated: local bar Grey's Saloon, Sage Carrigan's Copper Mountain Chocolates, the historic Graff Hotel and the tragedy-steeped River Bend Park.

Once we had our town of Marietta, Montana, we started writing about the people who live and love there, books that Tule Publishing branded *Montana Born*. I don't think any of us could have guessed back then how our readers would grow to love our town, how they would clamor for more stories, how they would wish they could visit or even move to Marietta themselves.

Over time more and more talented authors have written stories set in Marietta. The town has grown, and with each new story family trees are expanded and entwined. This book is a guide, for new readers and old, to enrich their *Montana Born* reading experience. On behalf of myself and the other founding authors of Marietta—Jane, Megan and Lilian—and the publishing team at Tule, I hope you enjoy your visit here.

C. J. Carmichael
Flathead Lake Cottage, May 2016

HISTORY OF MARIETTA

MARIETTA
CHAMBER OF COMMERCE

We're a quaint town located at the base of our beloved Copper Mountain. In the late 1800's copper was king and mining engineers from Butte found copper in our mountains and the rush was on, flooding Marietta with prospectors, miners and folks eager to get rich. But the copper in Copper Mountain was more like fool's gold, and in less than ten years, all copper mining in Marietta ceased.

From humble beginnings, Marietta grew into one of the finest towns in the state.

By 1899, many folks had left, but a few hardy souls stayed on, and gradually homesteaders and European immigrants started putting down roots, raising cattle, and working the land.

Today Marietta is a thriving community of ranchers, cattlemen, and commercial enterprise and we're proud of our colorful history. Every year we celebrate that history with the Copper Mt Rodeo, a three-day weekend festival variously held mid-September to the first weekend of October. There are bigger rodeos in America, and rodeos with bigger purses, but you won't find a rodeo anywhere with more heart.

Don't want to visit during our rodeo weekend? Come to Marietta and stay in one of our beautiful bed and breakfasts' or small inns and take in as much of Montana as you can.

In summer, hike up Copper Mountain, go zip lining or raft down Yellowstone River. Have kids? Check out the large Marietta City Park, just at the end of Main Street next to the Creamery – where you can get the best ice cream in all of Montana!

In the winter, enjoy skiing on the mountain, a fun sleigh ride through the hills, snowshoeing through the back country, ice skating on Miracle Lake or just cozy up and sit by the fire and read a great book.

Come visit us soon and see why Marietta, Montana has something for everyone, big and small.

The lower falls of the Yellowstone River.

Marietta Timeline

1872 – Yellowstone National Park created

1878 – Ephraim Grey builds and opens Grey's Saloon

1879 – Marietta formally incorporated with its first mayor and sheriff

1880 – Miners in Marietta; prospecting for silver and gold

1884 – Copper discovered

1885 – Railway to Marietta; Train brought in by Barton Dudley Crawford; Crawford also built the Marietta depot

1885 – Marietta Mountain renamed Copper Mountain

1884-1890 – Marietta's Building Boom: Crawford County Courthouse, Graff Hotel, Marietta Library, and St. James Church were all built during this period

1894 – Copper boom ends

1894 – 1905 – Decline of Marietta

1905-1920's – Transition to ranching and agriculture based economy

1938 – 1st Copper Mountain Rodeo

FOUNDING FAMILIES

The Grey / Crawford Family

Megan Crane

The Montana Greys have owned **Grey's Saloon** in Marietta, MT in one form or another since Ephraim Grey turned up in the area in the 1880s (after escaping some trouble in Boston as well as leaving behind his first and technically legitimate family: the Boston Greys) and started a saloon. His son and heir Josiah ran a bordello in the upstairs rooms, but it's been pretty much straight food and drink and the occasional gunfight since. Grey's Saloon is the oldest building in Marietta.

*   *   *

Here's a little on Barton "Black Bart" Crawford, Megan's character Chelsea's ancestor and one of Marietta's founders, who turned up in Marietta a bit later than Ephraim Grey (This and the quote below are from *Tempt Me, Cowboy*):

> "You're new here, so perhaps you don't know that the Crawford family was one of Marietta's First Families," she said reprovingly, aware that she sounded uncomfortably like her mother. That snooty intonation, even the way she was looking at him, as if the

name *Crawford* was branded into the side of Copper Mountain standing in the distance. Was this what she had to look forward to? Slowly becoming Mama? But she couldn't seem to stop herself, and the sad truth was that she knew the answer to that already. "Barton Dudley Crawford, my ancestor and one of Montana's great visionaries, brought the railway here in 18—"

"This railway?" he nodded toward the old railway line that ran behind the depot building, and unlike her history students, didn't look even slightly cowed when she scowled at him for interrupting her. "My railway?"

She didn't like his possessiveness, which was another sign she was becoming Mama much faster than she was comfortable with, so she opted to ignore it.

"The very same," she replied primly. "The Marietta Railway Depot is a symbol of our town's rich copper rush past, and stands as a monument to Barton Crawford as well as the many contributions of the Crawford family to this town and to this region since."

* * *

But the Greys were there first:

Grey's Saloon hunkered over the corner opposite her, complete with swinging doors on the front and that balustraded balcony running along the second story, where the prostitutes had displayed their wares back when Marietta was little more than an outpost and Grey's—the oldest building in town—was as much a bordello as a saloon.

Mama didn't like the fact that the Greys— purveyors of sin going back generations—were actually *more* original Mariettan than the Crawfords. *They make their presence known, don't they?* she always said when forced to acknowledge the existence of the saloon, or even the outdoor adventure outfit one of the other Grey brothers ran from an office above the town's bookstore.

Crawfords aren't flashy, Mama had told them over and over again growing up, despite the fact they lived in one of the area's historic old homes, rich in rambling, Victorian splendor up in the hills above the town. *Crawfords are genteel.*

It had taken Chelsea a long time to understand that what her mother meant was that the Crawfords had once had a great deal more money than anyone else had, and had fancied themselves many social classes above families like the Greys, hence their relocation out of the town proper. And that what they had left now was their heritage. And far too much pride.

Every now and again the weight of that heritage—and what it meant to her mother, and thus to Chelsea because she loved her mother and wanted to make her happy—made Chelsea feel flattened down to the ground beneath it.

The Parker Family

Michelle Beattie

Frontier Marietta begins in 1879 with Wade and Jillian's story. This is before the railroad has come to Marietta and before copper was found. The big mountain still overlooks the town but it's not called Copper Mountain at this time as the copper has yet to be discovered.

Like most things in history, towns looked quite different back in the 1800's than they do in modern days so other than Grey's Saloon, the Marietta you all know and love may be hardly recognizable. Other than Grey's the rest of the town is built of wood with lovely false fronts and wooden boardwalks of the time. You may recognize some familiar names but there are plenty of new ones as well. Here are a few characters you're most likely to see and meet in "Frontier" Marietta.

Wade Parker – Owns the Triple P Ranch

Jillian Matthews Parker – Town vet and Wade's wife (book 1)

Annabelle Parker – Wade's daughter from his first marriage

Eileen Parker Owens – Wade's mother

Shane McCall – Marietta sheriff and boyhood friend of Wade

Silver Adams – Another saloon owner of Silver's established after Grey's Saloon

The Carrigan Family /
The Bramble Family

CJ Carmichael

The Carrigans and the Brambles were both early settlers to Marietta. But while the Carrigans began and remained as hard working ranchers, the Brambles were an ambitious bunch who first made a fortune in copper mining, then experienced a series of twists and turns in their fortunes. Throughout all the hard times, however, the Brambles never lost ownership of their original home, one of the largest in Marietta, and now known as the Bramble House Bed and Breakfast.

The Bramble history begins with Henry and his wife May Bell who moved to Marietta from Boston in 1870. After earning their fortune in the copper mines (and rumor has it also discovering a vein of rare Montana sapphires) they built Bramble House. Before the mines dried up Henry invested in banks and railways.

Henry and May Bell had three children. Their twin girls, Pearl and Dorothy, died unmarried and under suspicious circumstances when they were 35 years old. Their son, John, (1875 – 1952) married Elizabeth. He continued the family mining business until the vein dried up in the early 1900's. After that he managed the family investments, suffering big losses in the thirties, after which time he dabbled in local journalism. John and Elizabeth had two sons, Chester (who died in World War I), and Warren. After marrying Isabelle, Warren made the best of what was left of the family's fortunes, as well as continuing in his father's tradition of journalism. Warren and Isabelle had three children:

- **Mabel** was born in 1929. She never married or had children and has lived at Bramble House all her life. In 2012 she was convinced by her great-niece Eliza that the great home should be converted to a bed and breakfast in order to make ends meet—a plan she has lived to regret. Mable continues to live in a suite on the main floor of the house.

- **Charles** was born in 1931 (and died in 2001) he married **Beatrice** and they had no children.

- **Steven*** was born in 1933 (and died in 2014). He worked for the local bank in Marietta and he and his wife, Cordelia, had three children:
  o **Bella,** their first, died as a baby
  o **John** married **Patricia** and they had four children:
    ▪ **Caro,** who was born in 1974, married Frank, and has no children
    ▪ **Hank,** who was born in 1978 remains unmarried
    ▪ **Steve,** born in 1980, also unmarried

- **Eliza,** born in 1982, the heroine of *Snowbound in Montana*, where she meets and falls in love with Marshall McKenzie

o **Beverly** was born in 1957. She married Hawksley Carrigan of the Circle C Ranch. They had four daughters and in 1996 Beverly died in a ranching accident.

- **Mattie** was born in 1975 and is the heroine of *Good Together* where she falls in love with **Nat Diamond.** Mattie and her first husband Wes Bishop had twin daughters **Portia** and Lauren **(Wren).**

- **Dani** was born in 1980 and is the heroine of *Close To Her Heart* where she falls in love with **Eliot Gilmore.** Dani and Eliot have a daughter Beverly and a son Joey.

- **Sage** was born in 1984 and is the heroine of *Promise Me, Cowboy* where she falls in love with **Dawson O'Dell.** They have a daughter **Savannah** (Dawson's from a previous marriage) and **Braden.**

- **Callan** was born in 1988 and is the heroine of *A Cowgirl's Christmas* where she falls in love with **Court.**

- *****Before** his marriage, Steven had an affair with **Judith Conrad** who had a son:

o **Greg Conrad** was born in 1951 and was raised by his mother, without any contact with his father. Greg married **Maeve** and they had four children. Their marriage ended in 2012. Greg and Maeve's four children are:

- **Finn Conrad** who was born in 1987, currently lives in Colorado, and is the hero of *A Bramble House Christmas* where he meets and falls in love with **Willa Fairchild**.

- **Molly** was born in 1985. She's married with two children and lives in Seattle.

- **Keelin** works as a psychiatrist in Seattle

- **Berneen** is the youngest and still lives with their mother

The Zabrinski Family

Debra Salonen

The Zabrinski family has deep roots in Marietta dating back to the mid-1880s when Royce Zabrinski, a Russian trapper, and wife, Jenny, a French-Canadian with Native American heritage set up trading. Jenny, whose real name was Geneveive, was beautiful and fearless. She knew how to shoot nearly as well as her husband. They only had one child.

Their son, Raford "Ray" (1875-1942) married Hilda (1877-1975), who the current generation refers to as their gypsy witch great-grandmother. Supposedly, she put a curse on a local banker who tried to cheat them and the man died two days later. It's believed that Hilda was a "negotiated" bride from the old country, brought west to marry Raford. Young, beautiful and a bit wild, Hilda never backed down from a challenge.

Ray and Hilda had eight children. Their first son died at birth, another was a failure-to-thrive baby. Of the six who lived, three were girls who married and moved away. Ray, Jr. died young, leaving no children. Rudolf, the youngest, was "not the marrying type" (gay). He moved back east to live with one of his sisters. Randolph "Ran" (1908-1978) became patriarch of the current Marietta family.

Randolph took over his parents' business after WWII. He had three sons: Richard, Robert and Roger. Richard died in a hunting accident in 1964. His only son, Jonathon, is father of Samantha (*Montana Miracle*). Robert and wife Sarah are parents to four Big Sky Maverick characters: Meg (*Maverick*), twins: Austen (*Cowboy*) and Mia (*Darling*), and Paul, who runs the Big Z Hardware (*Cowgirl*). Roger has one daughter, Katherine (*Montana Hero*). Roger lives in Malibu, California, and has nothing to do with the business, although he returns to Marietta often to see his grandson, Brady.

Other Big Sky Maverick players include:

Bailey Jenkins-Zabrinski, wife of Paul. They were high school sweethearts who parted under difficult conditions and reunited fifteen years later. Bailey is step-mother to Paul's two children: Chloe and Mark. Bailey and Paul, who married at the end of *Montana Cowgirl*, have a daughter together: Arya. Bailey owns and operates: B. Dazzled Western Bling.

Bailey's parents are Louise and OC Jenkins (*Montana Gift*). Louise is the children's librarian and published her first book—a memoir of her life with OC "The Fish Whisperer" Jenkins. Both are in their sixties.

Serena James is Austen's fiancée. She also raises alpacas, teaches a fiber class after school and works with children with auditory impairment. She bought the old Jenkins' place, which is next door to Austen's ranch.

Ryker Bensen married Mia Zabrinski on July 4th to the wonder and excitement of friends and family. Mia's two children from her previous marriage are Emilee and Hunter. Em is sixteen and looking into colleges. Hunter is into sports and video games. The whole family is dealing with two recent additions to their family (twins delivered via a surrogacy).

Henry "Hank" Firestone is a rancher Meg rescued (*Montana Maverick*) on Christmas Eve, along with his four, orphaned grandchildren: JJ, Annie, Bravo and Misty. Hank and Meg married after a short engagement, despite Meg's decision to become a surrogate for her sister and brother-in-law.

Ryker's brother, Flynn Bensen, moved to Marietta after a close call on the fire lines. Flynn accepted the job as head of Search and Rescue for the Crawford County Sheriff's Department. One of the first people he meets on the job is Katherine "Kat" Robinson, a single mom with a secret agenda that could create havoc in the Zabrinski family.

Kat is looking for the man who might be her birth father. She's narrowed down her search to one candidate: Robert Zabrinski. Since she's aware of how disruptive an unsubstantiated claim like hers might be to the family, she hadn't planned on sharing the information until she was certain. But her autistic son, Brady, has other plans.

Flynn's two best friends and fellow smoke jumpers, Tucker Montgomery and Justin Oberman, wind up in Marietta, too. Tucker decided to go "all in" and build a zip line in the mountains nearby. When he injures his ankle, he reaches out to Justin to keep the project going while Tucker handles the paperwork—and his beautiful roommate for the summer: Amanda Heller. Amanda—a temporarily unemployed NYC ad exec—is looking after her grandmother, Molly O'Neal – retired teacher and widow of Pat O'Neal, a life insurance guy, while Amanda's parents meddle with the estate and cause problems.

Justin is between jobs after the zip line closes for the season, so when an offer comes in from a company inviting him to help them develop a climbing apparatus to help physically-challenged people access the sport, he jumps at the chance—and the huge retainer they sent him. At Big Sky Maverick's premier New Year's Eve Masked Ball, he meets his dream girl, who turns out to be his new boss—and a girl from his past. Nikki Magnesson knows she and Justin have been set up by her "fairy-godfather" boss, J. Angus Hooper, but sharing one kiss with the man of her dreams opens up a world of possibilities.

In nearby, Paradise, Montana (the town that was promised the railroad—before Marietta won—some say "stole"— the line, Pastor Samantha "Sam" Zabrinski and her teenage daughter, Makayla, are recent transplants from Detroit, where Richard Zabrinski's son, Jonathon, was raised after

Richard's death. Sam always felt her heart belonged in Montana and once she meets Gage Monroe, she knows why.

I love my Marietta family, and I hope you do, too.

Deb Salonen

The Sheenan/Douglas Family

Jane Porter

The Douglas Family

Originally from Butte, Sinclair Douglas (1860-1930) arrived in Marietta in 1885 during the height of the copper mining boom to help manage Copper King Patrick Frasier's mining interests. In 1887 Sin Douglas warned Patrick Frasier of the deplorable—and dangerous—working conditions, insisting changes need to be made. Frasier brushed him off, not interested in investing more into a copper mine that isn't as profitable as he'd hoped, and Sinclair resigns. Less than a month later, a tunnel collapses, trapping dozens of miners. Sin leads the rescue party, and is able to save a dozen men, but five miners die in the tragedy. Knowing the accident was preventable, and disgusted by Frasier's greed, Sin leaves mining to raise cattle on his new property in rugged Paradise Valley.

In 1882, eighteen year old Copper heiress, McKenna Frasier (1864-1960), daughter to Patrick Frasier, one of the Butte Copper Kings, is sent from Butte to New York to attend college, travel, and be introduced to society. But when a scandal in December of 1888 destroys her reputation, her father disinherits her and McKenna's forced to take a job as a teacher, becoming the first teacher in Montana's Paradise

Valley.

Together, Sinclair and McKenna founded the Douglas Ranch of Paradise Valley. You can find their great-great-granddaughter, McKenna Douglas Sheenan, in Marietta today, along with McKenna's two older brothers, bull rider Rory and professional baseball player Quinn.

The Sheenan Family

The Sheenans trace their ancestry back to Irish immigrant, Seamus Sheehan, who arrived at Ellis Island from County Limerick in 1859. Just eighteen, Seamus leaves Ellis Island with papers, but they've inadvertently changed his name to Sheenan. Seamus doesn't really care one way or the other. He knows who he is, and he knows what he's come for and it's to earn money and help provide for his mam and brothers and sisters back home. Seamus makes his way to Texas where he works as a cow hand, and in 1866 is part of the Bozeman Trail cattle drive. Seamus ends up staying in Montana, and works for two years at the Frasier Copper Mine while homesteading in Paradise Valley, before leaving mining to ranch full-time.

KEY SETTINGS

Key Settings

Town of Marietta, MT

"There'd been nothing but the crisp blue dawn, the hint of the coming winter already there in the chill of the late September morning while Copper Mountain stood high above the town, a sleepy blue and purple giant slouching in the distance."

—*Tempt Me, Cowboy by Megan Crane*

"He took a moment to soak in the ambiance of Marietta, Montana. It was cool in the shade, but if you stepped into the sun you could almost believe you'd been transported back to summer. He liked the look of the park in front of the Courthouse. And the way Copper Mountain shone above the town, sunlight glinting off the granite facets.

It was a real town, solid and also beautiful."

—*Promise Me, Cowboy by CJ Carmichael*

"Marietta would have been a pretty town in any setting, with its classic Western store-fronts, but the mountains you could see in every direction made it truly beautiful. Above the square and solid fronts of Nineteenth Century Western-style buildings, you would suddenly see a row of rugged peaks, with streaks of snow still visible in the highest and most sheltered places."

—*Marry Me, Cowboy by Lilian Darcy*

"As usual her route took her along Bramble Lane, the nicest street in town, with stately brick and stone homes on one side and the Marietta River on the other. Many of the original mining magnates who had built this town on the profits of copper, had chosen this road for home.

Her own mother, Beverly Bramble, had descended from one of those families, and not only this street, but also the family home, still bore their name. Sage was passing it now, a red brick mansion on a stone foundation with white trim and a gracious porch. There was a turret above the porch and a widow's walk to the left of that.

When her mother was still alive, she used to take Sage and her three sisters to have tea with great-aunt Mabel once a month. That tradition had died, along with her mother, over fifteen-years ago. But great-aunt Mabel still lived on—now supported by a grand-niece who had turned most of the bedrooms in the old mansion into guest rooms...

Several blocks further on Bramble Road, past the mansions, were some more modest homes."

—*Promise Me, Cowboy by CJ Carmichael*

Description of the Valley outside of Marietta

"The drive to the Circle C was a long and beautiful one, winding along the valley that cut through the Gallatin Range to her right and the Absarokas to her left. Here there were miles and miles between neighbors. Most of the land was owned by just three families.

First were the MacCreadies, whose ranch house and outbuildings were about half-an-hour from Marietta. Mrs. MacCreadie was the sweetest woman, but she'd gone a little strange after the birth of her triplets—which had come just a year after her second child.

Fifteen minutes further she came to the Sheenan's spread. Bill and his wife had had a boy to match every one of the Carrigan girls, but they'd had very little to do with one another in school. Water rights were what it was all about when you were a rancher and Bill and her father had an ongoing feud about the mountain fed stream that ran along the border of their properties. They both had the right to use that water, but over the years both Bill and her own father had been guilty of some surreptitious damning and diverting.

Sage didn't know who had started it.

And she didn't care.

She had something else against the Sheenans…*secret number two.*"

—*Promise Me, Cowboy by CJ Carmichael*

Important Buildings

Courthouse:

"Across Crawford Park to the tall, domed courthouse dominating the public park, the stately courthouse, with snow-covered Copper Mountain rising behind it."

—*A Bramble House Christmas by CJ Carmichael*

Library:

"The library…built in the 1880's as the third public building constructed during Marietta's short-lived copper boom…with all those tall windows, the high ceilings, the marble foyer and staircase with hardwood floors on the first and second floors."

—*The Tycoon's Kiss by Jane Porter*

Popular Places in Town

Graff Hotel:

Graff Hotel

"After the two and a half year restoration.... the grand lobby glowed with rich paneled wood, marble, and gleaming light fixtures, while the grand ballroom and smaller reception rooms sparkled with glittering chandeliers."

—*The Tycoon's Kiss by Jane Porter*

Rocco's Italian Restaurant:

"Tuscan landscapes covered the faux plaster walls, with trompe l'oeil fountains and statues painted in corner niches. The ceiling featured a trellis with vines and clusters of oversized burgundy red grapes. Red-and-white-checked cloths covered each of the tables, topped by the obligatory red candle burning brightly in an empty Chianti bottle. The interior was a tad cliché, but at the same time, it exuded warmth and charm."

—*A Christmas Miracle for Daisy by Jane Porter*

Grey's Saloon:

"Grey's Saloon...complete with swinging doors on the front and that balustraded balcony running along the second story...the oldest building in town..."

—*Tempt Me, Cowboy by Megan Crane*

"The timeworn source of many Marietta, Montana, hangovers, Grey's had had the same decor for years – battered bar along one wall, booths along the other, scarred floorboards, tarnished mirrors."

—*Bound to the Bachelor by Sarah Mayberry*

Bramble House Bed and Breakfast:

"From the outside, the three-story Victorian—the largest home on the block and quite possibly in all of Marietta—looked both stately and welcoming. Fairy lights were strung along the eaves and porch railings and in the large front window, a Christmas tree glittered red, green and gold."

—*A Bramble House Christmas by CJ Carmichael*

"The historic B&B. There were lots of older homes lining the street but there was only one three story red brick mansion with elegant white trim and a big welcoming porch."

—*A Christmas Miracle for Daisy by Jane Porter*

Copper Mountain Chocolate Shop:

"Stepping inside, the first thing you'll notice is the scent—rich cocoa with vanilla, caramel and spice undertones. Mmm—so good. The cocoa and vanilla theme carry through to the decorating in the front showroom. The maple shelves are stained the color of forty-five percent milk chocolate and tiny vases with vanilla colored roses are displayed in a line on the feature wall. In keeping with the name of her store, Sage uses copper-tinted boxes for her chocolates, and these are arranged in attractive displays, delicious little pyramids of hand-made truffles, molded chocolates, and yummy granola bark.

Black and white photos on the wall behind the counter show every step of the chocolate making process. From buying the beans in Venezuela, roasting and cracking them in Sage's industrial grade kitchen, to conching, refining, tempering and finally molding."

—Promise Me, Cowboy by CJ Carmichael

Married in Marietta:

"Chandelier in the middle of the ceiling, pink velvet and brocade covered chairs, ornate free-standing mirror and white wicker glass topped counter with old-fashioned cash register on the countertop. Dress rails are around two walls and back of shop has two changing rooms with heavy curtains.

.... a huge amount of bouffant white and cream dresses. Everywhere he looked there was sparkle, flounce and lace. On an old-fashioned coat stand in the corner was a whole host of glittering veils. A shelf on the wall held a multitude of tiaras and on another, a whole variety of shoes and sandals."

—*The Fairy Tale Bride by Scarlet Wilson*

Java Cafe:

"He parked in front of the Java Café, and went inside, lining up at the counter to order a black coffee and an egg bagel sandwich.

The café was busy and he took a seat at a small table in the corner and read the Bozeman Daily Chronicle while he waited, and then ate the hot sandwich while pouring over the business section. He was still reading and nursing his second cup of coffee when the glass door swung open, bell jingling, and his brother walked in."

—*The Taming of the Bachelor by Jane Porter*

Main Street Diner:

"The walls were heavy red brick and the floor solid wood. There was a counter with red leather-covered stools bolted to the floor in front of it, and for as long as Carson could remember beehive-haired Flo was standing at the grill cooking delicious food, trading gossip, and flirting with any man who entered."

—A Cowboy for Christmas by Katherine Garbera

Fairgrounds:

"The fair itself was in full swing, with hordes of crowds coming through the turnstiles and packing the exhibit halls. Summer vacation was nearly at an end and Marietta's people were taking full advantage of the last vestiges of fun that August had to offer. From here, she could see the Ferris wheel spinning, hear the shrieks of fun being had on the midway, and smell the delicious wafts of fair food that traveled across the fairgrounds."

—*A Cowboy to Remember by Barbara Ankrum*

Rodeo Grounds:

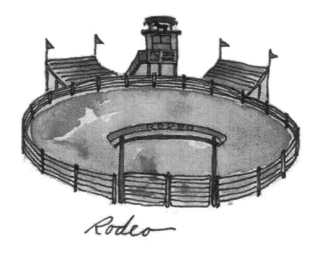

Rodeo

"The rodeo ground lay on the outskirts of Marietta, and looked like any of the scores of such grounds she had seen over the years. The yards and chutes and bleachers made of sturdy metal with peeling paint. The rodeo ring itself, thick with a pungent mix of sawdust and old manure and dirt. Clusters of modest-sized bathroom blocks and canteens and sheds. Open areas out the back that were already beginning to fill with pickups and trailers."

—*Marry Me, Cowboy by Lilian Darcy*

St. James Church:

St. James Church

"...before scooping up the train of her dress and walking away from him, heading for the entrance to the gray gothic-inspired St. James, the stunning Protestant church he'd never been in, because this wasn't his side of town."

—*Take Me, Cowboy by Jane Porter*

Hospital:

Hospital

"The patient had just been transferred to a level one facility. Thank goodness. Marietta Hospital dealt with emergencies as best it could – but it didn't have the facilities of a level one trauma center."

—*The Fairy Tale Bride by Scarlet Wilson*

Big Z Hardware and Lumber:

"Big Z Hardware is Marietta's 4th generation family-owned home improvement store where you can find everything for your home, garden, ranch and business, from agricultural supplies and barn door hardware to wheelbarrows and yard guard to keep away those pesky unwanted critters. Whether you're a DIY fix-it kind of person looking for just the right tools and material or someone in need of a professional to update your deck, bathroom or man cave, you'll find the answer to your home improvement needs with a quote from Big Z Hardware. And don't forget to check out Big Z's in-store outdoor adventure booth for all of your hunting, fishing, and hiking needs. Big Z's resident expert—the Fish Whisperer himself, OC Jenkins—will be on hand to teach the basics of fly-fishing, making flies, stream fishing, and gun safety."

—Debra Salonen

Marietta High School:

"She entered the school noting the hallways were lined with posters…announcing the theme of the Homecoming dance to be held later that night. She took a detour on her way to the cafeteria to peek into the gym.…she made her way to the cafeteria. The folding tables were down and lined in rows. Along one wall a line of electric griddles and pancake makers…"

"The Marietta high school stadium crackled with energy. Earlier in the evening a parade had marched through town, revving up the anticipation for the big game. Now the stands were filled with fans, most local from Marietta and a good portion from the visiting team of nearby Livingston High School. The two schools were huge rivals and that they were playing on the night of Homecoming upped the tension even more…"

—Home for Good by Terri Reed

Sweet Pea Flowers:

"She glanced at the window across her loft apartment. The florist's shop occupied the ground floor and she'd made this area into her home. It was full of wide open spaces…"

—*The Cowboy's Reluctant Bride by Katherine Garbera*

"She pushed open the door, revealing the backroom of the florist shop and a staircase up to the apartment. It smelled strangely earthy."

—*Bride by Mistake by Nicole Helm*

<u>Wolf Den:</u> "If she followed the train tracks down to the right she'd find the Wolf Den, the seediest bar in Marietta—which was helpfully located across the street from the old Catholic church and the police station, should the sins carried out within by the usually rough customers need addressing on either the spiritual or civic level."

—*A Game of Brides by Megan Crane*

<u>The Copper Mountain Gingerbread and Dessert Factory:</u>
"He entered the Copper Mountain Gingerbread and Dessert Factory as pleasant sounding chimes announced his arrival. Bakery smells of sugar and vanilla and flour fixed his sour mood. But no more than when Mindy Sue, dressed in pink with a polka-dotted apron, lifted her head from behind the counter, giving him a giant-sized smile."

—*Bachelor for Hire by Charlene Sands*

<u>Flintworks:</u> "Jonah tugged open the depot's front door and a cheerful burst of noise floated out to greet them as he ushered her inside...She knew that Jasper Flint had opened this microbrewery only a few months back, after painstakingly renovating the old train depot here in Marietta. But research and even detailed pictures on the Internet hadn't entirely prepared her for the appealingly clean lines and little touches that were obvious at first glance. From the big, bright paintings on the walls to the airy, open balcony seating area up above, every little detail was well thought out and gave the place a wide open, effortless feel.

Perfectly Montana, she thought. There were great steel vats behind high glass walls and a busy bar counter staffed by cheerful-looking bartenders in bright blue shirts. She saw a busy, open kitchen in the back and a menu written in a bold, welcoming hand across a chalkboard on the wall beside it."

—*Please Me, Cowboy by Megan Crane*

<u>Gallagher Christmas Tree Farm:</u> "The sealed road became gravel for a couple of hundred feet, then opened up into a sizeable parking area patronized by half a dozen cars. To one side was a rustic-looking log cabin, complete with cute little attic windows peeking out of the roofline, and to the other was a timber barn decked out in big red Christmas bows and flashing fairy lights. A couple of forty-gallon drums sat in front of the barn, the haphazard holes punched in their sides revealing fires burning within.

Cut Christmas trees were piled against one side of the barn, while others were dotted around, displayed upright thanks to half wine barrels that had been drilled centrally to create a sturdy stand. An elderly couple waited near the barn, while the rest of the customers walked amongst the trees, looking for the perfect specimen."

—*His Christmas Gift by Sarah Mayberry*

Landmarks:

Copper Mountain:

Copper Mountain

"There'd been nothing but the crisp blue dawn, the hint of the coming winter already there in the chill of the late September morning while Copper Mountain stood high above the town, a sleepy blue and purple giant slouching in the distance."

—*Tempt Me, Cowboy by Megan Crane*

Miracle Lake:

"A small lake close to downtown at the foot of Copper Mountain. Miracle Lake was a fancy name for what was essentially just a frozen pond in the middle of the woods ten minutes outside of town. In the evenings and weekends, kids would light a bonfire and roast marshmallows. During the day you could rent skates from the shack at the east end of the lake, or buy something hot to drink."

—*A Christmas Miracle for Daisy by Jane Porter*

Rural Ranch Community around Marietta

Even though these ranches aren't in downtown Marietta, they're still very important to the main characters, their families, and residents of the town. Enjoy getting to know a little bit more about them!

Anders Run: Next to Sweet Montana Farms, Roxanne Snopek

- Anders, Chad. Lives in the original house on Anders Run. Shares property with older brother, Eric. Runs charitable foundation Building Tomorrow. In *Cinderella's Cowboy* by Roxanne Snopek.
- Anders, Eric. Lives in renovated barn-mansion on Anders Run. Shares property with younger brother, Chad. Former bull-rider. Raises cattle, rough-stock. In *The Cowboy Next Door*.
- Plett, Leda. Lives with Eric Anders, at Anders Run. Has baby daughter, Hera. In *The Cowboy Next Door*.

Bar V5 Dude Ranch: Absaroka Rd, Melissa McClone
- Decker, Dustin. Wrangler.

- Harris, Zack. Wrangler, shooting instructor.
- Murphy, Ty. Co-owner.
- Murphy, Meg Redstone. Guest services and event planning.
- Randall, Charlotte "Charlie". Wrangler.
- Vaughn, Nate. Co-owner.
- Vaughn, Rachel Murphy. Owner: Copper Mountain Gingerbread & Dessert Factory, Main St.

Beargrass Hills Ranch: 540 Road, Alissa Callen
- Hollis, Payton. Owner.
- Morgan, Cordell. Agricultural consultant.
- Morgan, Ethan. Ranch hand.

Bluebell Falls Ranch: 540 Road, Alissa Callen
- Dixon, Kendall. Landscape designer.
- Dixon, Peta. Owner.
- Dixon, Rhett. Ranch hand.

Carlyle Stables: in *The Long Way Home* by Kathleen O'Brien
- Carlyle, Joe (hero, Abby's first love).
- Carlyle, Mary. Joe's widowed mom.
- Carlyle, Rafe. Joe's younger brother.

Circle C Ranch: Hwy 42 N, CJ Carmichael

- Carrigan, Hawksley. Owner: (deceased as of November 2014).
- Carrigan, Callan. Owner. Married to Court McAllister.

Circle K: on Timberline, Dani Collins

- Brady, Linc. Owner. Oil baron. Married to Meg Brady.
- Brady, Meg. Owner. Married to Linc Brady.

Copper Mountain Ranch: Absaroka Road, facing Copper Mt., in *Christmas at Copper Mountain* by Jane Porter

- Sheenan, Brock. Owner. Married to Harley Diekerhoff Sheenan.
- Sheenan, Harley Diekerhoff. Married to Brock Sheenan.

Dalton Orchard: Hwy 87. In *Almost a Bride* by Sarah Mayberry

- Dalton, Reid. Owner/manager. Police Officer, Bozeman, MT. Married to Tara Buck Dalton.
- Dalton, Tara Buck. Owner/manager. Police Officer, Bozeman, MT. Married to Reid Dalton.

Douglas Ranch: Hwy 87, Jane Porter

- Douglas, Rory T. Owner. Douglas Ranch.

Emerson Ranch: Hwy 42 N, in *What a Bride Wants* by Kelly Hunter
- Emerson, Ella Grace. Employee.
- Emerson, Samuel T. Owner.
- No Last Name, Carl. Ranch hand.
- No Last Name, Jem. Ranch hand.

Everett Ranch: Hwy 317, in *The Substitute Bride* by Kathleen O'Brien
- Everett, Butch (deceased).
- Everett, Drake. Owner.

Gallagher Ranch: in *Sing Me Back Home* by Eve Gaddy
- Gallagher, Dylan. Rancher.
- Gallagher, Wyatt. Orthopedic surgeon.
- Gallagher, Jack. Family practice doctor.
- Gallagher, Sean. Emergency room doctor.

Henley Ranch: in *Cinderella's Cowboy* by Roxanne Snopek
- Cash, Deirdre. (DeeDee). Aspiring model, assistant to stepsister Cynthia Henley. Maddie's fraternal twin.
- Cash, Madeleine. (Maddie). Assistant to stepsister Cynthia Henley. DeeDee's fraternal twin.
- Henley, Cynthia. Graphic designer, event planner.
- Henley, Joanie. (Formerly Cash) Mother of Madeleine and Deirdre. Married to Norm Henley.
- Henley, Norm. Owner, retired, leases out most of the land. Father of Cynthia. Married to Joanie (Cash) Henley.

High Country Mustang Ranch: Melissa McClone
- Killarney, Paddy. Owner.

KD Ranch: Hwy 89, in *For Love of a Cowboy* by Yvonne Lindsey
- Donovan, Kyle (Emmie). Owner.
- Lange, Booth. Foreman.

Lazy C: on Timberline, (which now has a spa B&B, very exclusive), in *Blame the Mistletoe* by Dani Collins
- Canon, Blake. Owner. Married to Liz Canon.
- Canon, Liz. Owner. Married to Blake Canon.

Lucky B Ranch: Paradise Valley, in *Bachelor for Hire* by Charlene Sands
- Matthews, Brand. Owner. Uncle of Cody (Code) Matthews.
- Matthews, Cody (Code). Ranch hand. Nephew of Brand Matthews. Ex-Army sergeant and security expert.

McCreadie Ranch: Copper Falls Road by Lilian Darcy
- McCreadie, Robbie. Owner. Married to Melinda McCreadie.
- McCreadie, Melinda. Owner. Married to Robbie McCreadie.
- McCreadie, RJ. Ranch hand.
- McCreadie, Jamie. Roughstock rider.

McCullough Ranch: Hwy 87, in *Last Year's Bride* by Anne McAllister

- McCullough, Sam. Owner. Married to Jane Weiss McCullough, father of Clint, Cole, and Sadie; also father of twins with Jane.
- McCullough, Clint. Architect. Father of Nick and Beatrix.
- McCullough, Cole (Nell). Owner.
- McCullough, Emily. Retired. Widow, mother to Sam McCullough.
- McCullough, Jane Weiss. Director, Marietta Chamber of Commerce, Main St. Married to Sam McCullough.
- McCullough, Nell Corbett. Film maker.
- Monroe, Levi. Started a rodeo school on McCullough Ranch.

O'Driscoll Ranch: Hwy 87 SE Marietta by Anne McAllister

- O'Driscoll, Shea. Owner.
- Tucker, Adam. Foreman, mountain guide.

Scott Ranch: Wash Creek Road by Katherine Garbera

- Davison, Monty.
- Scott, Alec. Part-owner.
- Scott, Carson. Owner.
- Scott, Hudson.
- Scott, Lane. USMC.

Sheenan Ranch: Hwy 89 by Jane Porter

- Sheenan, Bill. Late family patriarch – former owner Sheenan Ranch.
- Sheenan, Trey. Owner and manager.
- Sheenan, Dillion. Owner.
- Sheenan, Cormac. Owner.

Sweet Montana Farms: in *A Sweet Montana Christmas* by Roxanne Snopek

- Sweet, Austin. Farms honey on Sweet Montana Farms with wife, Melinda and baby son Abel.
- Sweet, Melinda. Farms with husband Austin on Sweet Montana Farms. Also a nurse-midwife.

Winslow Estate Thoroughbred Horses: in *Home for Good* by Terri Reed

- Locke, Matt. Part-owner.
- Winslow, Joelle. Part-owner.

THE SERIES OF
MONTANA BORN

WELCOME TO THE

COPPER MOUNTAIN

RODEO

The Copper Mountain Rodeo has been celebrated every year since 1938, and there are always cowboy reputations and love on the line. Come to Marietta for a three day festival held the first weekend of October. Main Street is always barricaded for a dance, famous country singers as well as local bands will be around to entertain, and don't miss the steak dinner to help raise funds for the community. The rodeo ain't for the faint of heart, so saddle up and enjoy the ride.

Books in the Copper Mountain Rodeo Series:

The 75th Copper Mountain Rodeo

Tempt Me, Cowboy by Megan Crane

Can an outsider convince a hometown girl that he means
to stay?

Jasper Flint – Owner, FlintWorks Brewery, Railway Depot
Chelsea Collier – Out to save old depot built by
her ancestors

Marry Me, Cowboy by Lilian Darcy

There's no chance it could turn into the real thing, because
they have nothing in common... do they?

Tegan Ash – Australian champion barrel-racer
Jamie MacCreadie – Rodeo rider

Promise Me, Cowboy by CJ Carmichael

Sage decides she's quitting the rodeo, and cowboys, but then
Dawson shows up after a five year absence. He says he's here
for her and he's making lots of promises. But can he
keep them?

Dawson O'Dell – Bronco rider, single father, and after
Sage's heart
Sage Carrigan – Chocolate shop owner, ex-rodeo rider
(Also book 1 in The Carrigans of the Circle C series)

Take Me, Cowboy by Jane Porter

What happens when the rodeo ends and Colton leaves town?
Will Jenny dare to dream again?

Colton Thorpe – Bull-riding champ
Jenny Wright – Executive assistant

The 76th Copper Mountain Rodeo

Tease Me, Cowboy by Rachael Johns

Levi doesn't want any distractions during his last rodeo, but
when his high school sweetheart comes along and offers to
rewrite their history, it might just be an offer too good
to refuse.

Levi Monroe – Rodeo rider and teacher
Selah Davis – Journalist in Seattle

Cherish Me, Cowboy by Alissa Callen

Can a sassy cowgirl lower her guard for a man who will soon
be gone? And can a man who believes emotions are nothing
but a liability take the ultimate risk?

Cordell Morgan – City boy
Payton Hollis – Working cowgirl

Kiss Me, Cowboy by Melissa McClone

Can Zack commit to love and convince Charlie not to leave? Or has she made up her mind to put the past, and the kiss that started it all, behind her and move on without him?

Zack Harris – Military veteran turned cowboy
Charlotte – aka Charlie – Randall – Dude ranch wrangler
(Also book 3 in the Bar V5 series)

Please Me, Cowboy by Megan Crane

Gracelyn and Jonah discover that in Marietta they just might find exactly what neither one of them was looking for…

Jonah Flint – Texas billionaire
Gracelyn Baylee Packard – Employed by Jonah, originally from Eastern Montana

The 77th Copper Mountain Rodeo

Claim Me, Cowboy by Charlene Sands

Will Ty seize his second chance and finally claim all that he's lost, including Summer's love, once again?

Tyler Warren – Rodeo rider
Summer Nichols – Runs Circle W Ranch

Hold Me, Cowboy by Alissa Callen

The shy and sweet Kendall Brent left behind has become a strong and determined woman. A woman who won't let her cowboy walk away for a second time.

Brent Ashton – Rancher and cowboy

Kendall Dixon – Strong, determined, Marietta hometown girl

Keep Me, Cowboy by Nicole Helm

Can Jess convince Cole, a wandering cowboy, that his home is with her?

Cole McArthur – Rodeo cowboy

Jess Clark – Helping Cole's foster family bring him home

Choose Me, Cowboy by Barbara Ankrum

Kate wants nothing to do with commitment, and sees helping Finn as a way of sealing off the hurt from her past. If they can just keep their hands off each other. But not if Finn has anything to say about it…

Finn Scott – Pro bull rider

Kate Canaday – Kindergarten teacher

(Also Book 2 in The Canadays of Montana series)

You're Invited
The Great Wedding Giveaway

The excitement is building in Marietta, Montana, with a series of stories centered around the 100th Anniversary of the Graff Hotel and—as part of the celebration—an incredible Wedding Giveaway.

The Graff Hotel has enlisted the entire town to stage a spectacular 100-year repeat of the Great Wedding Giveaway of 1914. Photographs and posters of the original event inspired a look back to an elegant time. Woodrow Wilson was President of the United States and King George V ruled England. High fashion drawings featured long skirts and elaborate feathered hats. As the dance craze swept the world, everyone was learning the tango... hemlines started to rise and "dance shoes" became popular.

Today's Great Wedding Giveaway seeks to recapture the style and grace of Marietta's past and launch a campaign to make Marietta a wedding destination. So couples from all over the country are invited to enter the contest and compete for the works—airfare, bridal gown, flowers, photography, food, the wedding suite at the Graff, a honeymoon, and more.

The stories in the Montana Born Brides series bring you the heart, humor, and charm of Marietta and the people who want to get married there (or not). Some brides are sweet, some are sassy, and all are as unique as Montana snowflakes. Watch for new releases... you won't want to miss a single one!

Books in the Great Wedding Giveaway Series:

What a Bride Wants by Kelly Hunter

Sawyer's the one Ella wants. But can he be the man she needs?

Cam Sawyer – Head of JB Beers, meets Ella as a bartender

Ella Grace Emerson – Works on Emerson Ranch

Second Chance Bride by Trish Morey

Mitch needs a wedding date, Scarlett needs money to fly home. It's a purely business relationship, or is it?

Mitch Bannister – Mining engineer

Scarlett Buck – Acts as Mitch's wedding date

Almost a Bride by Sarah Mayberry

Reid's a born wanderer, while Tara's roots run deep in Marietta. So even if things are good between them, it seems their romance is destined to be short and sweet…

Reid Dalton – Bozeman police officer

Tara Buck – Bozeman police officer

The Unexpected Bride by Joanne Walsh

Can she stay and do what she was hired to do without losing her heart in the process?

Laurent Fletcher – Widower, custom furniture maker

Emma Peabody – British nanny

The Cowboy's Reluctant Bride by Katherine Garbera

Monty as her knight in shining armor seems to be the last thing that Risa wants, so where does that leave him?

Monty Davison – Ex-Marine

Risa Grant – Florist, owns Sweet Pea Flowers in Marietta

(Also book 3 in the Scott Brother series)

A Game of Brides by Megan Crane

Can a wedding fling between two people become something more? If so, how can Emmy walk away from the one man she's always loved now that she knows what she's been missing?

Griffin Hyatt – Owner of Griffin Flight, extreme sports hero
Emmy Mathis – Disgruntled graphic designer

The Substitute Bride by Kathleen O'Brien

Jilted and pregnant, Marly is back in Marietta. But is Drake's sweet and caring act just a show for the papers?

Drake Everett – Rancher at Everett Ranch
Marly Akers – Reporter at Copper Mountain Courier

Last Year's Bride by Anne McAllister

Married for less than a year, Nell is not ready to give up on their marriage. Cole is stubborn, but they will soon find out exactly what they are willing to do for love.

Cole McCullough – Rancher at McCullough Ranch
Nell Corbett – TV director

Make-Believe Wedding by Sarah Mayberry

It's the perfect solution to an accidental entry into the wedding giveaway, except Heath very quickly realizes that pretending Andie is his is no hardship at all. In fact, it may just be the best thing that's ever happened to him...

Heath McGregor – Owner of McGregor Construction

Andie Bennett – Electrician

Start your bidding!

Bachelor Auction

★ Grey's Saloon ★
Saturday Night

Each year, Marietta buzzes with anticipation as the annual Bachelor Auction approaches. What's not to love about raising money for a good cause, while indulging in red-hot fantasies, as some seriously sexy Montana men man-up and take the stage for a fun show and offer creative dates for the lucky bidders?

Grey's Saloon has hosted the Bachelor Auctions. The first year gave readers six brave men of Marietta who flexed and strutted and smiled to raise money for young Josh Dekker, who had sustained serious injuries in a fall while camping and hiking. Beau, Ryan, Linc, Jett, Jesse and Gabriel stole the spotlight and introduced their lucky ladies to dream dates that included everything from skiing adventures to gourmet meals and handyman skills to wine tasting. These men had it all.

Not to be eclipsed, hometown bachelors Code, Nick,

Colt and Gavin, former Marietta Grizzlies football players, reunite and step up to help their retired coach launch a foundation to improve the local hospitals' helipad after Coach D's grandson died during an unlucky tackle at a home game. These dates offer everything from a romantic weekend getaway that includes a wedding, to a 101 on protection detail for a famous actress, to a lady's choice date that has one bachelor finally coming home and imaging a happily ever after.

The stories in the Montana Born Bachelor Auction series bring you the heart, heat, and heroes of Marietta guaranteed to charm and entice as couples flirt, clash and come together. All the bachelors and their dates have pasts and challenges, and watching the sparks smolder into a blaze makes it nearly impossible to put any of the books down. Watch for new releases coming... you will want to read them all!

Books in the Bachelor Auction Series:

Year 1

Bound to the Bachelor by Sarah Mayberry

As Beau does his best to keep Lily safe, they discover that maybe they don't dislike each other quite as much as they thought. In fact, maybe it's just the opposite...

Beau Bennett – Owner of Copper Mountain Security

Lily Taylor – Admin at Wade Printing

Bachelor at Her Bidding by Kate Hardy

When the attraction between Ryan and Rachel flares, they both discover that they just might dare to love again. Then tragedy strikes, pushing them apart. Can Ryan possibly win Rachel back... with cake?

Ryan Henderson – Top pastry chef
Rachel Cassidy – Doctor

The Bachelor's Baby by Dani Collins

This is a one-night thing. One night that turns into nine months and maybe a lifetime...?

Linc Brady – Millionaire, owner of Circle K Ranch
Meg Canon – TV journalist in Chicago

What a Bachelor Needs by Kelly Hunter

No strings, no sex, no commitment. Just fix things. Surely it can't be that difficult...

Jett Casey – Ski champion
Mardie Griffin – Waitress at Grey's Saloon, single mom

In Bed with the Bachelor by Megan Crane

As far as Jesse is concerned, Michaela is forbidden fruit. But how long can he resist the one woman he shouldn't touch?

Jesse Grey – one of Seattle's foremost construction tycoons, Jason Grey's nephew

Michaela Townsend – Chief administrative officer for tech tycoon in Seattle

One Night with Her Bachelor by Kat Latham

Will Molly and Gabriel's never-quit attitude have them rushing head-first into love? Or will Gabriel's secret pain stall their relationship before it can get off the ground?

Gabriel Morales – Former Air Force pararescueman

Molly Dekker – Kindergarten teacher, mom of Josh Dekker

(Also book 1 in the Wild Montana Nights series)

Year 2

Bachelor for Hire by Charlene Sands

Spending their weekend date in a remote cabin, Cody plays the role of reluctant bodyguard, yet Hayley isn't going to let the tormented man deny his feelings for her, no matter the threat to her body or her heart.

Cody Matthews – Ex Army sergeant and security expert, lives on Lucky B Ranch

Hayley Dawn O'Malley – Hollywood starlet

Falling for Her Bachelor by Robin Bielman

A deal's a deal, but when their "business transaction" turns into more pleasure than duty, can they walk away from each other without losing what matters most?

Nick Palotay – Navy firefighter

Cassidy Ware – Photographer

Seducing the Bachelor by Sinclair Jayne

As Colt and Talon burn up the sheets, he begins to forget why he hates this town, and Talon wonders if she can learn to trust enough to fall in love. But will that be enough to convince him to stay?

Colt Ewing – Special Forces sniper

Talon Reese – Veterinary student, single mom

Weekend with Her Bachelor by Jeannie Moon

Is Gavin and Ally's story just beginning, or will their romance end with the weekend?

Gavin Clark – Emergency doctor

Ally Beaumont – Event planner in Seattle

THE
Big Marietta Fair

GET YOUR TICKET
TODAY!

Grab your cotton candy and hop on the Ferris wheel for a bit of summer love. The Big Marietta Fair is in town! Marietta is full of handsome cowboys, and whether or not they're chasing love, it will find them at the annual fair. Old flames will be reignited, and new friends may discover there just might be more to it than that. Buy your tickets and get in line for the most anticipated event of the summer... and love's waiting at the Big Marietta Fair.

Books in the Big Montana Fair series:

Beauty and the Cowboy by Nancy Robards Thompson

Jesse has harbored a serious crush on Charlotte since her beauty pageant and high school days, but she was always unavailable, and now that her relationship status just might be single, he intends to hang onto this chance and ride to the end of the bell.

Charlotte "Charlie" Morgan Guthrie – former beauty queen, now Jane Weiss's assistant at the Marietta Chamber of Commerce

Jesse Guthrie – former professional bull rider, now runs the Marietta Fair Grounds

Montana Cowgirl by Debra Salonen

The love of his life broke his heart and made him hate her...or so he thought. The line between love and hate is very narrow, with only so much room for forgiveness. If anyone is capable of building a bridge for them to cross together, it's him.

Paul Zabrinski – Owner, Big Z Hardware and Lumber

Bailey Jenkins – Owner, B. Dazzled Western Bling

(Also Book 1 in the Big Sky Mavericks series)

For Love of a Cowboy by Yvonne Lindsay

Life is simple for Booth Lange until Willow Phillips arrives in Marietta and turns his entire world upside down. At first, it seems she's everything he can't stand and yet, he can't seem to stay away...

Booth Lange – Works in Marietta, gives Willow a ride to town

Willow Phillips – Superstitious, hippie, looking to connect with the father she's never met

Her Summer Cowboy by Katherine Garbera

Will the sweet summer nights at the country fairs and a burning attraction to a tempting songstress teach Hudson how to stop running and how to build a life with a woman he just might be falling in love with?

Emma Wells – Professional musician

Hudson Scott – Cowboy who lives life on the road

(Also book 2 in the Scott Brothers of Montana series)

A Cowboy to Remember by Barbara Ankrum

Olivia resolves to keep Jake at arm's length, even though the memory of his kisses keeps her up at night. She knows better than to let her heart get involved, but Jake is planning for the future. Their future. Can Jake convince her to risk it all one more time and really make this a fair to remember?

Jake Lassen – Ex-Army helicopter pilot, owner of a helicopter company

Olivia Canaday – Ex-Olympic equestrian hopeful, teaches dressage to area kids

(Also book 1 in the Canadays of Montana series)

Marietta

Homecoming

Go Grizzlies!

It's homecoming week and the alumni from Marietta High are all returning to their roots… and some will unexpectedly find love along the way. Bundle up for the football game and don't miss the bake sale, but most importantly return to the good old days with the heroes of Marietta, Montana as they win back former loves and discover what's been hiding right under their noses.

Books in the Homecoming series:

Sing Me Back Home by Eve Gaddy

Can a mad, passionate affair last or will it burn itself out as quickly as it began?

Dr. Jack Gallagher – Family practice doctor, single father

Maya Parrish – Former model, Owner of Maya's Models, single mother

Finding Home by Roxanne Snopek

Logan's determined to pull out all the stops to prove to Samara and her daughter that he's a guy they can count on. But, despite how easy it is to love Logan, second chance is still a gamble Samara can't afford to take

Logan Stafford – Marietta High School teacher, restores derelict Marietta heritage

Samara Davis – Widow, single mother, currently unemployed teacher

(Also book 1 in the Montana Home series)

Hometown Hero by Dani Collins

Chase wants her to join his fast-paced, larger than life world, but Skye¹s a small town girl at heart. Can she convince him that Homecoming is more than a game, and he's back where he belongs?

Chase Goodwin – Professional baseball player

Skye Wolcott – Secretary

The Long Way Home by Kathleen O'Brien

The years have changed Joe, too…and the passionate, powerful man he's become isn't someone Abby will ever forget. This time the heart she breaks may be her own.

Joe Carlyle – Rancher at Carlyle Stables

Abby Foster – Paralegal

Home for Good by Terri Reed

Can he convince the dark haired beauty to not walk out on him and her home for a second time?

Matt Locke – Part-owner, Winslow Estate
Thoroughbred Horses

Joelle Winslow – Jewelry designer, part-owner of Winslow Estate Thoroughbred Horses

You're invited...

Montana Born Brides

To the wedding of the century!

Wedding fever has hit the little town of Marietta... in addition to being taken over by a rowdy reality television crew. A celebrity bride is in town, and the bridal salon is getting its best business yet. Join the heroes and heroines of Marietta's Montana Born Brides series as they help plan the wedding of the century, and discover their own happily ever afters.

Books in the Montana Born Brides series:

The Fairy Tale Bride by Scarlet Wilson

As he spends more time with her, sparks fly, and he realizes that he's not the only one in Marietta with secrets…

Adam Brady – New doctor at Marietta Hospital, covers all departments

Lisa Renee – Owner of Married in Marietta Bridal Salon

His Blushing Bride by Dani Collins

They agree to a no strings affair, but will they wind up tying the knot?

Sebastian Bloom – Political science doctoral candidate

Piper Tierney – Marietta High School music teacher

Bride by Mistake by Nicole Helm

One night together has permanent consequences, and this time Beckett knows he can't outrun his bad boy reputation. He's determined to make Kaitlin his bride…even if he has to seduce her down the aisle.

Beckett Larson – Co-owner of Shuller Automotive

Kaitlin Shuller – Floral designer, Luke Shuller's sister

Finally His Bride by Maisey Yates

When the dust settles, will she get thrown back into the friend zone, or will she finally get the man of her dreams?

Luke Shuller – Co-owner of Shuller Automotive, Kaitlin Shuller's brother

Melanie Richards – Wedding cake designer

Kiss the Bride by Rachael Johns

It's not just the music Magdalena awakens. For the first time in a long time, Jake feels alive again and wants more out of life, starting with her. But there's more to Magdalena than meets the eye.

Jake Kohl – Country music singer

Magdalena Davis – Wedding singer, single mom

Two Nights with His Bride by Kat Latham

Wyatt has two nights in the wilderness to show her what a real man looks and acts like. A rugged, tough, loving man. But will he be able to do it before she says "I do" to the wrong man?

Wyatt Wilder – Owner of Wild Montana Adventures

Nancy Parsons – Soap opera star

(Also book 2 in the Wild Montana Nights series)

Carrigans of the Circle C

CJ Carmichael

Hawksley Carrigan, owner of the Circle C Ranch south of Marietta, Montana, always wanted a son to carry on the family name. Unfortunately for him, he ended up with four daughters.

Dear Reader,

Is it possible for one weekend to change your life?

Yes. And that's exactly what happens when the Copper Mountain Rodeo comes to Marietta, Montana this year.

In my story Sage Carrigan, local chocolatier, is going to have to decide whether she can forgive cowboy Dawson O'Dell for a terrible mistake he made five years ago.

I had a lot of fun packing this story with some of my very favorite things. Like gorgeous mountain scenery. Characters to root for, and characters to drive you crazy. And chocolate! Sage, who owns Copper Mountain Chocolate, creates all her products from scratch. I'd always wondered how to make chocolate and what my research told me was—

it isn't easy. Thank goodness there are so many wonderful chocolatiers who are willing to do all that hard work for us!

What else is in the book? Well, it's a reunion story, which is one of my favorite types of romances... especially when they involve a cowboy with a wild past who is willing to change his ways for the right woman.

Chapter one awaits... I hope you enjoy. And please come back for more stories about the Carrigans Of The Circle C. I'm working on them right now!

Happy Reading,
CJ

Books in the Carrigan of Circle C series:

Promise Me, Cowboy (Sage Carrigan's story)

Sage decides she's quitting the rodeo, and cowboys, but then Dawson shows up after a five year absence. He says he's here for her and he's making lots of promises. But can he keep them?

Dawson O'Dell – Bronco rider, single father, and after Sage's heart

Sage Carrigan – Chocolate shop owner, ex-rodeo rider

Good Together (Mattie Carrigan's story)

For anyone who has ever pondered what it means to be married, or had to reinvent her life when one breaks down. It's about having your heart broken but being strong enough to survive and love again…

Mattie Carrigan – Mother of twins Portia and Wren, and dealing with a cheating husband
Nat Diamond – Rancher, and friend, next door

Close to Her Heart (Dani Carrigan's story)

Is it possible that Elliot, Dani's next-door neighbor and friend, hasn't been playing the field–but waiting for her?

Dani Carrigan – Psychology professor
Elliott Gilmore – Divorce attorney

Snowbound in Montana (cousin Eliza Bramble's story)

Christmas is looking like a write-off for Eliza Bramble, until Marshall McKenzie suggests they make the best of what they have, and work together. Soon she realizes Marshall isn't just fixing Christmas—but her broken heart, too.

Eliza Bramble – Runs Bramble B&B
Marshall McKenzie – Owner of Grizzly Adventures
in Marietta

A Cowgirl's Christmas (Callan Carrigan's story)

For years Callan Carrigan has been her father's right hand man, so when her dad's will names city slicker Court McAllister the new owner of the Circle C Ranch, Callan feels betrayed on every level. But if she agrees to be foreman at the Circle C for one year, he'll deed the ranch back to her and her sisters. The deal seems too sweet at first—until Callan realizes Court has his eyes on something she protects even more than her family's land—her heart.

Callan Carrigan – Helps run the Circle C Ranch

Court McAllister – City slicker, new owner of Circle C Ranch

A Bramble House Christmas

Finn Knightly a.k.a. Finn Conrad is travelling to Bramble House B&B in Marietta to find answers. Instead he finds Willa Fairchild and her six-year-old son Scout, who quickly steal his heart.

Finn Knightly / Conrad – Looking for answers about his deceased father

Willa Fairchild – Mystery woman involved somehow with Finn's father

Big Sky Mavericks

Debra Salonen

Books in the Big Sky Maverick series:

Montana Cowgirl

The love of his life broke his heart and made him hate her…or so he thought. The line between love and hate is very narrow, with only so much room for forgiveness. If anyone is capable of building a bridge for them to cross together, it's him.

Paul Zabrinski – Owner, Big Z Hardware and Lumber

Bailey Jenkins – Owner, B. Dazzled Western Bling

Montana Cowboy

Even at first glance, Serena can tell Austen is nobody's cowboy, but who's to say that isn't a good thing? A little tryst with her sexy neighbor might be the perfect welcome to Montana.

Austen Zabrinski – Attorney, owner, The Flying Z Ranch
Serena James – Alpaca rancher

Montana Darling

When beautiful Mia shows up and orders him off what she says is her land, Ryker realizes she might be the spark he needed to jumpstart his interest in living again.

Ryker Bensen – Photographer, author
Mia Zabrinski – Attorney, single mother

Montana Maverick

Meg is forced to accept that falling in love with Henry and his ready-made family would require her to abandon her dream. Can this "Lone Wolf" assimilate into a new pack, or is this Big Sky Maverick meant to be alone?

Henry Firestone – Rancher
Meg Zabrinski – Scientist, environmental advocate, and tenured professor

Montana Hero

Will Flynn be the hero Kat needs to help her find the courage to fall in love again?

Flynn Bensen – Head of Crawford County Search and Rescue

Kat Robinson – Employee of Crawford County Search and Rescue

Montana Rogue

Roommates with benefits. A temporary arrangement between two people with time on their hands. Who could possibly get hurt?

Tucker Montgomery – Businessman Mountie's Marvelous Montana Zip Line and Enduro Course, project manager

Amanda Heller – Advertising executive

Montana Miracle

Sam has no intention of giving up on Gage Monroe–a man with depth and heart he hides from the world. Besides, Gage just may be the Christmas miracle Sam's been praying for…

Gage Monroe – Handyman, single father

Samantha Zabrinksi – Pastor, single mother

Montana Rebel

A kiss at midnight with her very own Prince Charming isn't too much to ask, is it? But what are two star-crossed lovers supposed to do when one kiss isn't enough?

Justin Oberman – Head of Climb Above, project with The Masters Group

Nikki Magnesson Richards – Executive assistant, J. Angus Hooper's executive assistant

The Taming of the Sheenans

Jane Porter

If you've read my books before, you know I love connected stories, and have written numerous series featuring families for Harlequin Presents, Grand Central Publishing and Berkley Books. The Taming of the Sheenans, is my brand new series about six powerful wealthy brothers from Marietta, Montana and boy oh boy do these men know how to take over a scene and own the room! The Sheenans are big, tough, rugged men, and as different as the Montana landscape.

xoxo Jane

Books in the Taming of the Sheenan series:

Christmas at Copper Mountain

When sparks fly and the attraction sizzles between Harley and Brock, Harley's not so sure she can handle something permanent with this dark, taciturn cowboy who doesn't know how to let her in. But Brock is determined to hold on to her and praying for a Christmas miracle...

Brock Sheenan – Owner of Copper Mountain Ranch, father of Mack and Molly Sheenan, oldest Sheenan brother

Harley Diekerhoff – Temporary housekeeper of Copper Mountain Ranch, widow from CA

The Tycoon's Kiss

Can Taylor turn a cold shoulder to Troy's heart-melting charms, or is this about to be Marietta's hottest Valentine's Ball yet?

Troy Sheenan – San Francisco technology tycoon, owner of the Graff Hotel, twin brother Trey Sheenan

Taylor Harris – Librarian

The Kidnapped Christmas Bride

Once again, Trey risks everything, but this time it's for love….and the memory of one perfect Christmas together as a family.

Trey Sheenan – Resident bad boy, manager of Sheenan Ranch

McKenna Douglas – Photographer at Big Sky Photography, mom of TJ Douglas (Sheenan), lost family in a tragedy

The Taming of the Bachelor

One date—and an incredibly hot kiss—with Dillion Sheenan wakes Paige up and makes her dream again. Until she finds out Dillon's already bought his ticket out of town… Is Dillon about to break the heart of the only woman he's ever loved?

Dillon Sheenan – Biomedical engineer in Austin, TX, youngest Sheenan brother

Paige Joffe – Owner of Main Street Diner, single mom

A Christmas Miracle for Daisy

He's not at all ready to settle down, and he's definitely not getting back together with his old flame, so Santa can stop playing matchmaker as it'd take a miracle to make him fall in love, never mind marriage material. But that's exactly the kind of miracle our angelic Santa Claus has planned...

Cormac Sheenan – Publisher/Owner of *Sheenan Media,* guardian of Daisy Davis

Whitney Adler – Creative director for Sheenan Media, Daisy Davis' godmother

The Lost Sheenan's Bride

Normally Shane would never use a woman, but if Jet can connect him with the keys to his past, he doesn't seem to have a choice. Until he begins to fall for her. Can two strangers, who were never meant to be, believe in love again?

Shane Swan (Sheenan) – Writer

Jet Diekerhoff – Teacher, Harley Diekerhoff's sister

The Scott Brothers of Montana

Katherine Garbera

Hello Marietta Readers!

When Jane Porter first told me about Marietta I fell in love. I wanted to live in the small town and in my mind I do. I see the Scott Ranch and the diner where the Scott brothers eat each Wednesday night. I'm from a small town myself so I totally understand the love/hate relationship that develops when you grow up in such a small place. I couldn't wait to leave my own small town and some of my characters share that desire. They want to get out in the big world and prove themselves. Test themselves away from the safety of their family and friends. Other characters run away from the small town and from mistakes and regrets but they always come back home.

I love returning to Marietta in the books I write about the Scott brothers and in reading the stories of the other authors. And speaking of Scott brothers...readers, I promise you, Lane Scott's story is coming. He's such a special hero that his story has taken some time but I am as anxious as you for it to be written and for Lane to have his happily-ever-after.

Happy reading!
Katherine

Books in the Scott Brothers of Montana series:

A Cowboy for Christmas

Being trapped together during a December snowstorm gives Annie and Carson a chance to rekindle their romance, but is Annie back for good or is she just looking for a cowboy for Christmas?

Annie Prudhomme – Returned to Marietta to find her roots
Carson Scott – Single father, forester who provides the town with their Christmas trees

Her Summer Cowboy

Will the sweet summer nights at the country fairs and a burning attraction to a tempting songstress teach Hudson how to stop running and how to build a life with a woman he just might be falling in love with?

Emma Wells – Professional musician
Hudson Scott – Cowboy who lives life on the road

The Cowboy's Reluctant Bride

A knight in shining armor seems to be the last thing that Risa wants right now, though he knows it's what she needs, so where does that leave Monty?

Monty Davidson – Ex-military, Marine hero

Risa Grant – Florist owner in Marietta

Cowboy, It's Cold Outside

Lucy isn't crazy about the holidays, so Trey does his best to restore her enthusiasm, starting with nestling her snug in his bed. But if he's only in town until New Year's…

Trey Scott – Photojournalist

Lucy Demarco – Cafe owner, entrepreneur

Bar V5 Ranch

Melissa McClone

The History of Bar V5 Ranch

In 1909, the Enlarged Homestead Act increased the size of a homestead plot from 160 acres to 320 acres. Nathaniel Vaughn, who had been working as a ranch hand, took advantage of this and struck a claim that he worked with his younger brother Nicholas. The two farmed the land and added a few heads of cattle. In 1916, the stock raising Homestead Act increased the size to 640 acres of grazing land. Nicholas took advantage of this increase to expand the size of their land holdings by adding cattle. The brothers named the combined acreage the Bar V5. Nathaniel's son, Victor, took advantage of the Great Depression to expand the Bar V5 holdings. He also inherited Nicholas' portion of the ranch, when the man died unmarried and childless in 1952. Victor worked with his son Ralph until his retirement. Ralph's son Nate, a venture capitalist, took over the Bar V5 from his father and turned the cattle ranch into a working dude ranch. In 2014, the dude ranch became a year round operation and bears little resemblance to the original ranch built so many years ago.

"She'd visited the Bar V5's website to check out where her brother worked, but the photographs didn't capture the beauty and grand scale of the ranch house. The architecture made her think of a mountain lodge—high-end, luxurious accommodations—not a place where cowboys and guests in hats and spurs drank beer and ate at plank tables after a long day on the trail. "I get the appeal. Christmas card perfect.""

—Home for Christmas by Melissa McClone

"Josiah stared out the passenger seat window. The setting sun created a watercolor of blues, pinks, yellows, and oranges in the sky. The two-story log structure looked more like a five-star, luxurious mountain lodge than a working dude ranch. Twinkling, white lights decorated the eaves. A single candle flickered inside each wood-pane window. Garland, tied with red ribbon, hung from the porch railing. A huge wreath, full of pinecones and holly berries, graced the front door.

Hallmark movie perfect. His idea of a living hell."

—A Christmas Homecoming by Melissa McClone

Books in the BarV5 Ranch series:

Home for Christmas

Is mixing business with affairs of the heart a recipe for disaster? Or will all of Rachel's wishes come true?

Nate Vaughn – Co-Owner, Bar V5 Dude Ranch
Rachel Murphy – Owner, Copper Mountain Gingerbread and Dessert Factory

Mistletoe Magic

All Noah wants now is to maneuver the pretty preschool teacher under the mistletoe. But if he's not careful, he'll wind up on Santa's naughty list.

Noah Sullivan – Veterinarian, Copper Mountain Animal Hospital
Caitlin Butler – Preschool teacher

Kiss Me, Cowboy

Can Zack commit to love and convince Charlie not to leave? Or has she made up her mind to put the past, and the kiss that started it all, behind her and move on without him?

Zack Harris – Military veteran turned cowboy
Charlotte – aka Charlie – Randall – Dude ranch wrangler
(Also Book 3 in The 76th Copper Mountain Rodeo series)

Mistletoe Wedding

Meg is not interested in a romance with a cowboy like Ty, or any man. Getting her under the mistletoe is going to take a Christmas miracle . . . or a little help from Santa.

Tyler Murphy – Co-owner, Bar V5 Dude Ranch

Meg Redstone – Event planner, single mother

A Christmas Homecoming

After a simple kiss under the mistletoe, Ellie and Josiah both start questioning everything. Can Christmas really bring the gift neither one of them were expecting: true love?

Josiah Whittaker – CEO, Whit Tech

Ellie Smith – Housekeeping, Bar V5

River Bend

Lilian Darcy

Books in the River Bend series:

Late Last Night

Late that night, after prom is over, a tragedy at River Bend
Park brings Kate and Harrison together yet again, and this
time, in the highly charged atmosphere, Kate discovers that
she never wants to let him go. But with his divorce still fresh,
is Harrison ready for someone new?

Harrison Pearce – Sheriff
Kate MacCreadie – English teacher at Marietta High School,
aunt to Jamie MacCreadie

The Sweetest Thing

Has he forgiven Tully for leaving him in the lurch on prom
night? And is there any chance that he and Tully can

6666

rekindle what they might once have had, when he's still tied to someone else?

Ren Fletcher – Attorney at Fletcher Law Office
Tully Morgan – Movie studio senior accountant in Los Angeles, Suzanne "Sugar" Morgan's daughter

The Sweetest Sound

Despite the sparks that fly between them, she and Charlie couldn't possibly be serious about each other, when they're committed to lives on opposite sides of the Atlantic Ocean… could they?

Charlie Barnett – Orthopedic surgeon, "Sugar" Morgan's son
Ramona Garrido-Lopez – Musician

After the Rain

That's how you stop being angry at someone when they're gone. You channel your anger onto the man you hold responsible, the man who's right here, no matter how heart-stoppingly gorgeous he is.

Casey "Jay" Brown – Architect for Haraldsen Foundation
Kira Shepherd Blair – Office manager for Haraldsen Foundation, single mom, Neve Shepherd's sister

Long Walk Home

But Gemma's secrets have been rusted up inside her for so long that not even a gorgeous man like Dylan Saddler can help her to break them free.

Dylan Saddler – Businessowner, single dad
Gemma Clayton – Teacher at Marietta High School, single mom

Montana
Home
Roxanne Snopek

Dear Reader,

I grew up with parents who loved do-it-yourself home improvement projects, so even though I'm a novice, I was thrilled to write a series with this backdrop. At the moment, my husband and I are deep in our very first do-it-yourself project: retiling our kitchen backsplash. So far, we've had no emergency room visits and we're still speaking kindly to each other, so we're counting it a huge success!

The main characters in the four novellas of MONTANA HOME are all involved in a restoration project of some kind, either rediscovering the beauty in a derelict heritage house or turning an old barn into a showpiece or even bringing an entire farm back to life. And while they're at it, they're also fixing something broken within themselves. My opinion? Repairing drywall is easier than facing our own mistakes. But in renovations and relationships, the only way to the reward is through good, old-fashioned work.

Thanks for spending time in MONTANA HOME.

You're always welcome here!

Roxanne Snopek

PS: You wouldn't believe the mess we made in our kitchen, but it turned out so great! To see photos, go to facebook .com/RoxanneSnopekAuthor and tell me what you think!

Books in the Montana Home series:

Finding Home

Logan Stafford never forgot the lonely girl from the wrong side of the tracks who broke his heart. Not only is she as irresistible as ever, but her delightfully odd little girl has him wrapped around her finger in no time. Believing they've been given a second chance, Logan's determined to pull out all the stops on the house to prove to them both that he's a guy they can count on.

Logan Stafford, high-school teacher in Marietta, part-time construction foreman
Samara Davis: special-needs teacher, widow, transplanted from New York City

A Sweet Montana Christmas

Austin's not-so-sweet side rears up as he determines he's done trying to make everyone happy. He'll get his wife back this Christmas no matter what. And they'll decide their future together.

Austin Sweet, former investment advisor, farmer
Melinda Sweet, maternity nurse, farmer

The Cowboy Next Door

Rodeo-star turned agent Eric Anders can't stand it that some jerk has left Leda high and dry. Clearly, the boots-and-sundress wearing mouthy mama needs someone on her side. He could change her life, if only she would let him. Can she trust the cowboy next door?

Leda Plett, high-school drop-out and new mother, taken in by Melinda and Austin Sweet
Eric Anders, former rodeo champion and sports agent, now rancher and philanthropist

Cinderella's Cowboy

When playboy-rancher Chad hires Cynthia, she's got a chance to shine. Professionally, at least. Until she learns of his fascination with a mysterious dream-girl. Cynthia knows she's no man's dream-girl and never will be. But there's magic at the ball. Princesses glow in the starlight, princes appear out of nowhere, and, sometimes, they look a lot like cowboys...

Cynthia Henley, owns her own public relations company

Chad Anders, rancher, philanthropist

Wild Montana Nights

Kat Latham

Dear Reader,

What do you get when you combine the stunning Montana landscape with three strong-willed brothers and women who desperately need a fresh start in life? Plenty of opportunities for some wild Montana nights, that's what!

When I think of Marietta, I immediately picture a close-knit community with all the things that are most important in life—friends and families who would do anything for each other. And that's exactly what I've found with the community of Montana Born readers and authors. Thank you from the bottom of my heart for reading my stories. Please let me know what you think of them. I hope you enjoy them!

Happy reading!
Kat

Books in the Wild Montana Nights series:

One Night with Her Bachelor

Will Molly and Gabriel's never-quit attitude have them rushing head-first into love? Or will Gabriel's secret pain stall their relationship before it can get off the ground?

Gabriel Morales – Former Air Force pararescueman
Molly Dekker – Kindergarten teacher, mom of Josh Dekker

Two Nights with His Bride

Wyatt has two nights in the wilderness to show her what a real man looks and acts like. A rugged, tough, loving man. But will he be able to do it before she says "I do" to the wrong man?

Wyatt Wilder – Owner of Wild Montana Adventures
Nancy Parsons – Soap opera star

Three Nights Before Christmas

Working together challenges every assumption Lacey and Austin have about each other, and they discover a desire hot enough to melt even the deepest Montana snow.

Austin Wilder – Forest ranger
Lacey Gallagher – Freight train engineer

Wildflower Ranch

Alissa Callen

Dear Reader,

Welcome to my small corner of Paradise Valley where the wildflowers bloom and the cowboys and cowgirls ranch the land of their forefathers. In my Wildflower Ranch series each ranch was named by its pioneering family after a local wildflower. Just like the Montana wildflowers that endured fire, drought, snow and flood, the pioneers too had to find a way to survive in a sometimes unforgiving land.

Generations later the fight for survival continues. For some of the descendants it now is a deep loneliness they may face, a broken heart or the need to find someone to stand shoulder to shoulder with through life. So come and share their journeys in my Wildflower Ranch series where hearts are healed, dreams are realized and the pain of the past is eased by the promise of the future.

Alissa

Books in the Wildflower Ranch series:

Cherish Me, Cowboy

Can a sassy cowgirl lower her guard for a man who will soon be gone? And can a man who believes emotions are nothing but a liability take the ultimate risk?

Cordell Morgan – Agricultural consultant, Ethan's twin brother

Payton Hollis – Owner of Beargrass Hills Ranch

(Book 2 of the 76th Copper Mountain Rodeo series)

Her Mistletoe Cowboy

The more time Ivy spends with the workaholic, blue-eyed cowboy next door the more she realizes her heart isn't actually broken – yet.

Rhett Dixon – Ex-rodeo rider, ranch hand Bluebell Falls Ranch, siblings Kendall and Peta

Ivy Bishop – Corporate analyst

Her Big Sky Cowboy

But when the summer ends, has time run out not only for Finn but also for Zane? Can the reserved cowboy find the words to make strong-willed Trinity stay… forever?

Zane Nash – Rancher, Finn's uncle
Trinity Redfern – Speech therapist, owner of Chatterbox
Speech Therapy

His Outback Cowgirl

The biggest challenge Ethan must face is to accept how
Bridie makes him feel. And the biggest risk Bridie must take
is to trust in her heart.

Ethan Morgan – Ranch hand at Lakespur Ridge Ranch,
Cordell's twin brother
Bridie Willis – Australian cowgirl

Hold Me, Cowboy

The shy and sweet Kendall he left behind has become a
strong and determined woman. A woman who won't let her
cowboy walk away for a second time.

Brent Ashton – Rancher
Kendall Dixon – Landscape designer at Bluebell Falls Ranch,
siblings Rhett and Peta
(Also book 2 of the 77th Copper Mountain Rodeo series)

His Christmas Cowgirl

As tinsel drapes Main Street Marietta, has Peta left it too late to show the man she loves the woman beneath the dust and the denim? And has the rancher who refuses to listen to his heart realized too late that success is hollow unless he has a certain stubborn cowgirl by his side?

Tanner Ross – Ranching tycoon

Peta Dixon – Runs Bluebell Falls Ranch, siblings Rhett and Kendall

The Davis Sisters

Rachael Johns

When Jane Porter emailed and asked if I'd like to write a rodeo story for Montana Born Books, I was so excited. I read the first rodeo series (75th Copper Mountain Rodeo) last year when it first came out and fell in love with small-town Marietta. Since then I've devoured as many of the novellas set in Marietta as I can, many written by authors I've admired for years. So it's a privilege to find my own home in Marietta and bring you my first Montana Born story— TEASE ME, COWBOY.

As with most stories, the seeds of this one have been germinating in my mind for a while now, waiting for the perfect moment. It mostly started with a conversation on Twitter where one author said she would like to tell her younger self to enjoy herself more and experiment with more men. As I'm a sucker for first-love stories, I thought about giving my heroine this regret also. And thus, Selah Davis, the "good" daughter of the church minister in Marietta, was born.

I had such fun writing this novella (in which Selah and her first-love cowboy, Levi Monroe, return to Marietta for the rodeo, and Selah's best friends dare her to proposition him), and I hope you'll enjoy reading it just as much! Do let me know what you think on Twitter or Facebook.

Happy reading,
Rach!

Books in the Davis Sister series:

Tease Me, Cowboy

Levi doesn't want any distractions during his last rodeo, but when his high school sweetheart comes along and offers to rewrite their history, it might just be an offer too good to refuse.

Levi Monroe – Rodeo rider and teacher

Selah Davis – Journalist in Seattle

(Book 1 of the 76th Copper Mountain Rodeo)

Kiss the Bride

For the first time in a long time, Jake feels alive again and wants more out of life, starting with Magdalena. But there's more to Magdalena than meets the eye.

Jake Kohl – Country music singer looking to get out of the spotlight

Magdalena Davis – A single mom who fled town fifteen years ago when she was a pregnant teen

A Year of Love in Marietta

Dani Collins

Dear Reader,

I live in a small town so each of my Marietta books has been a love letter to this wonderful life I enjoy. I can say with complete honesty that towns do exist where people are this kind and supportive of each other. And yes, people can occasionally be as nosy, too. (I'm not sure, however, if towns exist with this many marriageable-aged hot bachelors and sexy virgins!)

The interconnected community of Marietta feels authentic, though, don't you think? It feels real. It operates like a real community, too. Often I see authors posting within our writing groups about where their character might shop for a particular item, (in my case a maternity bra for Meg,) or asking if someone has a child in one of their stories who could be a friend of a new character's son. We almost need building permits, too, since we nearly erected too many gyms for this small town to support.

Like the real life town I inhabit, I moved into Marietta

without realizing how deeply I would fall in love with it and every day I thank my lucky stars I *am* here.

I also arrived in Marietta knowing I wanted to write a series, but not quite conceptualizing it ahead of time. So many authors are great at linking their books through a common theme or a mystery or a family history. My stories tend to be a slightly less organized connection of friends and siblings each forming their own little square in the quilt of many colors that is Marietta.

So far I've written four Marietta books and have a fifth set in Glacier Creek, Montana, coming out in June of 2016. (*Scorch*, in the Smokejumper series!) It ties to my Marietta stories, though. Watch for it and you'll get a little visit with Piper and Sebastian from His Blushing Bride.

I'm also hoping to get a sixth written this year, another Christmas book, set in Marietta so my characters can do the stroll. Like everyone who visits this warm and welcoming little town, I never want to leave!

I definitely hope to see *you* there.

Take care,
Dani

Books in the Year of Love in Marietta series:

Hometown Hero

Can she convince him that Homecoming is more than a game, and he's back where he belongs?

Chase Goodwin – Major league baseball player
Sky Wolcott – Secretary at Marietta High School

Blame the Mistletoe

It's the beginning of a new view of Christmas for Liz, but when their children arrive home unexpectedly, and family secrets are revealed, Liz isn't sure she'll stay in Marietta for Christmas after all.

Blake Canon – Owner of Lazy C Ranch, father of Ethan Cannon, brother to Meg Canon
Liz Flowers – Runs high-end spas in California, mother of Petra Flowers

The Bachelor's Baby

This is a one-night thing. One night that turns into nine months and maybe...a lifetime?

Linc Brady – Millionaire, owner of Circle K Ranch
Meg Canon – TV journalist in Chicago, sister to Blake Canon

His Blushing Bride

They agree to a no strings affair, but will they wind up tying the knot?

Sebastian Bloom – Political science doctoral candidate, Liz Flowers' brother

Piper Tierney – Marietta High School music teacher

The Canadays
of Montana
Barbara Ankrum

Books in the Canadays of Montana series:

A Cowboy to Remember

Olivia resolves to keep Jake at arm's length, even though the memory of his kisses keeps her up at night. She knows better than to let her heart get involved, but Jake is planning for the future. Their future. Can Jake convince her to risk it all one more time and really make this a fair to remember?

Jake Lassen – Ex-Army helicopter pilot, owner of a helicopter company
Olivia Canaday – Ex-Olympic equestrian hopeful, teaches dressage to area kids

Choose Me, Cowboy

Kate wants nothing to do with commitment, and sees helping Finn as a way of sealing off the hurt from her past. If they can just keep their hands off each other. But not if Finn has anything to say about it…

Finn Scott – Pro bull rider

Kate Canaday – Kindergarten teacher

READER FAVORITES

A reader-made list of favorite spots in Marietta!

Places

- Sage's Chocolate Shop for guilty pleasures
- The Main Street Diner and the old-timers who eat there
- Grey's Saloon for onion rings and a drink
- The Graff Hotel for special occasions
- Bramble House is a cozy B&B in Marietta
- Flintworks is a microbrewery with delicious food
- Down to the picnic tables by the river to watch the water
- The bridal shop to find a beautiful dress on sale
- The Java Cafe to get a good cup of coffee
- Copper Mountain Gingerbread and Dessert Company to get all of your favorite holiday treats; especially the gingerbread

Events

- Christmas in Marietta
- The Bachelor Auction
- The Fair
- The Rodeo
- The Gingerbread competition

- The Christmas Stroll
- Homecoming

To join other readers who love Marietta as much as you do, request to be a member of the group here!
www.facebook.com/groups/553178244849422

COLORFUL MARIETTA CHARACTERS AND FUN READER TRADITIONS

Colorful Marietta Characters

- Carol Bingley....town gossip
- Owner of the Bramble House B&B, Mabel Bramble, crusty great-aunt of the Carrigan girls and of Eliza Bramble, speaks her mind (and then some). All the Carrigan girls dread going to visit, but tea with Great-Aunt Mabel is a Christmas tradition.
- Em McCullough, Cole and Clint McCullough's grandmother, who bakes a mean rhubarb delight, is always there when you need her, directed the Marietta Christmas pageant for fifty years, and in a former life, confessed to having been a Radio City Music Hall Rockette
- Flo from the diner
- Gruff, embattled Sam McCullough, Em's son, who after years of having sworn off marriage, has met the love of his life in Jane Weiss
- Kris Krinkle – Santa in A Christmas Miracle for Daisy
- Nell of Nell's Cut 'n' Curl – Hairstylist extraordinaire of the silver heads in town
- The hands from Brock Sheenan's ranch

Join us!
The Christmas Stroll
First weekend in December – Downtown Marietta

Every year Marietta, Montana holds its popular Christmas 'stroll,' fashioned after the Bozeman Christmas Stroll.

Bozeman's stroll is held the first weekend of Dec (held that weekend to help drive retail sales) so Marietta's is the weekend after so as not to compete, but we could easily push it back until closer to the holidays.

All the info for the Marietta Stroll was adapted from Bozeman's.

On Saturday, December 6th (in 2016 this will be Saturday, December 3rd) from 4:30 to 7:30 PM join the Downtown Marietta Association as we proudly present the 30th Anniversary of the Christmas Stroll in Historic Downtown Marietta!

Come kick-off the Holiday Season in Downtown Marietta!! Join us for fun activities, great food, and fun. Bring the whole family to ride on the hay wagons, get your picture taken with Santa Claus, watch the lighting ceremony of the downtown decorations, check out the gingerbread house contest entries, sing Christmas carols, grab a bite to eat from one of over 30 non-profit food vendors or do some Christmas gift shopping. The Christmas Stroll is the place to find it all!

The Christmas Stroll is a free community event that is 100% supported by our business sponsors and the sales of our timeless button souvenirs. You can support this great event by purchasing a $3 Stroll button, which is not only your ticket to enjoy many of the great activities including the Santa pictures at the Graff Hotel, the hay wagon rides, kid's activities throughout the day at the Courthouse and the Marietta Library and more, it also allows us to put on this great event every year without requiring an entry fee!

Buttons will be available after November 22nd (in 2016 this will be November 19th) at the following locations:

- Main St Diner
- First Bank of Marietta
- Mercantile
- Main St Shoes
- Java Cafe
- Florist
- Copper Mountain Chocolates
- Hair salon(s)
- Marietta Public Library
- Gift Store(s)
- Graff Hotel

- Marietta Chamber of Commerce
- Copper Mountain Gingerbread and Dessert Co.

Along with all the fun activities listed below...our hay wagon rides are a great way to make timeless memories with family and friends at the Christmas Stroll. We could not bring you this incredible activity without the help of our generous sponsors.

- 4:30 PM Santa leaves the Rodeo Fair Grounds, travels down Front Ave to 5th St, meets the hay wagon at the intersection of 5th Street and Main Street, and leads the lighting ceremony down Main Street to the Courthouse in Crawford Park
- 4:30 – 7:30 PM Main Street is filled with food vendors raising money for local non-profits organizations
- 4:30 – 7:30 PM Downtown businesses feature live music, free cocoa and cookies, and holiday fun of all sorts
- 4:30 – 7:30 PM First Bank of Marietta on 1st and Main is displaying the 2014 Gingerbread House Contest entries and winners
- 4:30 – 7:30 PM Hay wagon rides from Crawford Park (in front of the library) to the Rodeo Fair Grounds and back
- 4:30 – 7:30 PM Stop by the Bridger Bowl booth (located in front of the Mercantile on Main Street) to learn about

their new and great plans for this year's ski season!

- 5:00 – 7:30 PM Santa pictures at the Graff Hotel. Get one FREE picture through Marietta Photography

RECIPES

Beverages

Copper Mountain Hot Chocolate

Ingredients

- 2 cups half-and-half or whole milk
- 4 ounces of Sage's bittersweet chocolate, finely chopped
- 4 ounces of Sage's milk chocolate, finely chopped
- Tiny pinch of salt
- ½ teaspoon freshly ground cinnamon

Directions

1. Warm ½ cup of the half-and-half or milk, then slowly add the chopped chocolates and salt, stirring until the chocolate is melted. Do not allow to boil.

2. Once the above mixture is smooth slowly whisk in the remaining half-and-half or milk, heating until the mixture is warmed through (but not boiling). Add the cinnamon.

3. Use a hand-held blender, or a frother, and mix the hot chocolate until it's completely smooth. Pour into a mug that has been warmed with boiling water.

Top with whipped cream and chocolate curls.

Mountain Berry Bachelor Martini

From Grey's Saloon specialty Bachelor Auction drinks

Ingredients

- 2 oz Teton Huckleberry Vodka*
- ½ oz Triple Sec
- ½ oz cranberry juice
- ½ fresh lime
- Twist of candied ginger or fresh ginger
- Ice
- 3 fresh or frozen huckleberries for garnish

Preparation

1. Take chilled martini glass and rub squeezed lime half around the rim.
2. Dust rim of glass with cocktail sugar.
3. Shake vodka, Triple Sec, cranberry juice and fresh squeezed lime juice in a cocktail shaker with ice for at least 30 seconds.
4. Strain into prepared martini glass.
5. Garnish with three huckleberries (fresh in season or frozen) on a cocktail stick.
6. Add candied ginger to the rim.

* Plain vodka works as well, but then you might want to muddle ¼ of huckleberries (or other berries) and strain into the cocktail shaker along with the vodka, Triple Sec, Cranberry juice and lime juice.

Marietta Bachelor Berry Margarita

From Grey's Saloon specialty Bachelor Auction drinks

Ingredients

• Three ripe strawberries, a small handful of blueberries and a small handful of huckleberries (fresh is best but frozen works fine/other berries can be substituted)

• 1 oz simple syrup*

• 2 oz fresh lime juice

• Lime zest

• 2 oz tequila

• ½ oz Grand Marnier

Preparation

1. Make a small amount of lime zest and press out any moisture with a paper towel then mix in with a bit of cocktail sugar.

2. Run a wedge of lime around the rim of the margarita glass and dip glass in cocktail sugar.

3. Add berries, simple syrup and Grand Marnier (other liquors work as well) in glass and muddle (strain out seeds if seeds will bother you in the drink).

4. Add tequila and lime juice and swirl in glass.

5. Add ice cubes (ice can be crushed and drink can be blended if you prefer).

6. Garnish with lime wedge and a sliced strawberry on the rim.

* Simple syrup can be purchased or made by adding equal parts sugar and distilled water and then heated until sugar is fully dissolved.

Side Dishes

Grandma Bramble's Cranberry Coleslaw

Ingredients
- Shredded cabbage
- Shredded apple
- Shredded carrots
- Dried cranberries
- Toasted almond slivers
- Apple cider vinegar
- Canola oil
- Maple syrup
- Dijon mustard
- Celery seeds
- Salt
- Pepper

Directions
1. Toss into salad bowl:
- 4 cups shredded cabbage
- 1 cup shredded apple
- A cup shredded carrot
- ½ cup dried cranberries

- ½ cup toasted almond slivers

2. Mix together dressing:

- ¼ cup apple cider vinegar
- ¼ cup canola oil
- 2 TBSP maple syrup
- 2 TBSP Dijon mustard
- 1 tsp celery seeds
- Salt & pepper to taste

3. Toss salad with dressing and refrigerate until ready to serve. Enjoy!

Entrées

Main Street Diner's Cinnamon-Apple Pork Chops

Who wouldn't want to eat at Marietta, Montana's Main Street Diner? Check out their Cinnamon-Apple Pork Chop recipe and be sure to stop by and visit Paige Joffe (when is that girl not working?).

4 Servings
Prep/Total Time: 25 min.

Ingredients

- 2 tablespoons reduced-fat butter, *divided*
- 4 boneless pork loin chops (4 ounces *each*)
- 3 tablespoons brown sugar
- 1 teaspoon ground cinnamon
- ½ teaspoon ground nutmeg
- ¼ tablespoon salt
- 4 medium tart apples, thinly sliced
- 2 tablespoons chopped pecans

Directions

1. In a large skillet, heat 1 tablespoon butter over medium heat. Add pork chops; cook 4-5 minutes on each side

until a thermometer reads 145 degrees. Meanwhile, in a small bowl, mix brown sugar, cinnamon, nutmeg and salt.

2. Remove chops; keep warm. Add apples, pecans, brown sugar mixture and remaining butter to pan; cook and stir until apples are tender. Serve with chops. Yield: 4 servings.

While your oven pre-heats, **start reading** Book 4 in the Taming of the Sheenans series, Paige and Dillion Sheenan's story, by NYT and USA Today bestselling author Jane Porter!

Logan's Favorite Meatloaf

In FINDING HOME, Logan Stafford cares for a very wounded and guarded heroine by feeding her, and Roxanne Snopek says, it's one of her favorite scenes! This meatloaf was a household favorite when their kids were small and since her real life hero loves it, she figured her story hero would too. Enjoy!

Ingredients
- 1 cup old-fashioned oatmeal
- 1 package dry onion soup mix
- 1 cup grated carrots or zucchini
- ¾ cup ketchup
- 2 eggs
- 2 tsp salt
- ½ tsp pepper
- 2 lbs lean ground beef
- ½ cup water
- 1 cup grated cheddar cheese (optional)

Directions
1. Stir oatmeal and onion soup mix together. (You can grind the oatmeal in a food processor first, if you want.)
2. Add the grated carrots or zucchini, ketchup, eggs, salt, pepper and water and mix well.

3. Add beef and mix until thoroughly combined.

4. Pack into 2-quart casserole. Bake uncovered at 350° for 1-1 ½ hours. Sprinkle with cheese and return to oven just long enough to melt, if desired.

Serves 6-8.

Chance Watson's Last Chance Pulled Beef

Ingredients

- 2-3 pound piece of brisket
- Olive oil
- 1 head of celery
- 2 brown onions
- Handful of fresh rosemary sprigs
- 2 bay leaves
- 1 lemon
- 1 700g jar passata or homemade tomato sauce
- 2 tbs Worcestershire sauce
- Teaspoon chipotle sauce
- 2 tbs maple syrup
- 4 cups beef stock

MASH

- 2-3 lb potatoes
- 2 tbs horseradish chopped fine

Directions

1. Heat oven to 250° F, Place casserole dish over high heat.
2. Season brisket all over and place in pan with a slug of olive oil. Brown all over.
3. Chop celery and onions, add to pan, reduce to low heat until vegetables softened.

4. Juice the lemon and add to pan.

5. Add passata and other ingredients with beef stock. Bring to a boil and turn off heat. Cover the pan with tinfoil or lid and place in the oven for 5-6 hours.

6. Cook potatoes in boiling water, drain and mash with a dob of butter and splash of milk, stirring in the horseradish.

7. Pull meat apart with two forks and serve on a plate with sauce.

8. Serve over mashed potatoes.

Desserts

Em McCullough's Rhubarb Delight

Em does this mostly by trial and error—and she has made it for years and years, so she has a pretty good success rate. It tastes fantastic—all the kids, grandkids and great-grandkids love it. Give it a try.

Ingredients
- Flour
- Margarine or butter
- Powdered sugar
- Sugar
- Eggs
- Salt
- Rhubarb

Directions
Preheat oven to 375 degrees.

1. Crumble together:
   - 1 c flour
   - ½ c margarine or butter, cut in pieces
   - 3 TBSP powdered sugar
   - (Em uses her hands to crumble this. You can use a

fork if you're feeling fastidious.)

2. Set aside ½ cup of above mixture.

3. Pat the rest of the mixture into the bottom and sides of a 9" pie pan. Don't go up over the edges of the pan (just up the sides) because the butter will make it burn if it's exposed when the filling is in it and you put it back in to bake longer. Bake crust 10 minutes at 375. When finished baking, set on rack to cool.

4. While the crust is baking, mix together:
   - 1 ¼ c sugar
   - 2 eggs beaten
   - pinch of salt

5. Add:

6. 2 ½ c rhubarb, chopped fine, to the above mixture.

7. Pour the sugar, egg and rhubarb mixture into the cooled crust in the pie pan.

8. Sprinkle the reserved ½ cup of crumbled unbaked crust mixture over the top.

9. Bake about 35 minutes at 375.

The top should be golden in places and the filling should be set so it's fairly firm, not sloshing around in the pan. If it sloshes, leave it in the oven longer.

Cool before serving. Refrigerate whatever you have left (Em rarely has any left).

If you have need to serve more people, you can double the recipe and make two pies or you can put the doubled mixture in a 9" by 13" pan. You may have to adjust amounts—so why don't you follow Em's recipe first until you've got the hang of it

Em McCullough is the grandmother of Cole McCullough of *Last Year's Bride* and of Clint McCullough of *McCullough's Pride*, both of whom have a distinct fondness for it. She also makes this recipe for Shea O'Driscoll in *O'Driscoll's Heir* by Anne McAllister.

Sage Carrigan's Chocolate Date Cake
Home Sweet Cowboy (The Chocolate Shop Books)

Ingredients
- 1 cup dates, pitted and chopped
- 1 cup boiling water
- 1 ¾ cups all-purpose flour
- 1 teaspoon baking soda
- ¼ teaspoon salt
- 3 teaspoons unsweetened cocoa powder
- 1 cup white sugar
- ½ cup butter
- 2 eggs
- ½ cup chopped walnuts
- 1 cup semisweet chocolate chips, divided

Directions
1. In a small bowl, combine dates with boiling water. Set aside to cool.
2. Preheat oven to 350 degrees F (175 degrees C).
3. Grease and flour a 9x13-inch pan.
4. In a medium bowl, mix flour, soda, salt and cocoa. Set aside.
5. Cream butter and sugar until light and fluffy.
6. Add eggs. Add flour mixture alternating with cooled date

mixture. Fold in chopped nuts and ½ cup of the chocolate chips to mixture.

7. Spread batter into prepared pan. Sprinkle remaining ½ cup of chocolate chips over top.

8. Bake in preheated oven for 45 to 60 minutes, or until toothpick inserted into middle of cake comes out clean.

Rachel Vaughn's Gingerbread People

Ingredients
- ¾ cup packed dark brown sugar
- 1 stick butter or margarine, softened
- 2 large eggs
- ¼ cup molasses
- 3 ¾ cups all-purpose flour
- 2 teaspoons ground ginger
- 1 ½ teaspoons baking soda
- ½ teaspoon ground cinnamon
- ½ teaspoon freshly grated nutmeg
- ½ teaspoon salt
- 1 cup confectioners' sugar, sifted
- 1 to 2 tablespoons milk
- Food coloring, as desired

Directions
1. At low speed, cream sugar and butter until thoroughly combined.
2. Add eggs and molasses. Mix until combined.
3. Sift together flour, ginger, baking soda, cinnamon, nutmeg, and salt.
4. Add the dry ingredients to butter mixture and combine with a spatula.

5. Remove dough from bowl; wrap in plastic wrap. Refrigerate until firm, about 1 hour.

6. Preheat the oven to 350 degrees F. Line cookie sheets with parchment paper.

7. Allow the dough to sit at room temperature for about 15 minutes.

8. Take ½ cup of dough at a time and roll onto a floured board until about 1/8-inch thick.

9. Cut out with gingerbread boy and girl cookie cutters.

10. Transfer the cookies from the board to the prepared cookie sheets. Bake for 10 minutes, until just beginning to brown at the edges.

11. Transfer to wire racks to cool.

12. To make the icing, combine the confectioners' sugar and milk.

13. Divide mixture into thirds; leave 1/3 white, and color 1/3 green and the final third red.

14. Decorate piping eyes, mouths, buttons, and bow ties.

Gingersnap How-To from Liz of Blame the Mistletoe

Ingredients

- 1 ½ c white sugar
- 1 c butter or margarine
- 2 eggs
- 1 c molasses
- 1 Tbsp baking soda
- 2 tsp baking powder
- 1 Tbsp ground ginger
- 4 c flour
- 1 tsp ea: nutmeg, cinnamon, cloves, all spice

Directions

1. Cream together:
2. 1 ½ c white sugar
3. 1 c butter or margarine
4. Add:
5. 2 eggs
6. 1 c molasses
7. Sift together in a separate bowl:
8. 1 Tbsp baking soda
9. 2 tsp baking powder
10. 1 Tbsp ground ginger

11. 4 c flour

12. 1 tsp ea: nutmeg, cinnamon, cloves, all spice

13. Stir dry ingredients into wet

14. Roll dough into balls 1 inch in diameter

15. Dip top into white sugar

16. Place on greased cookie sheet – Do Not Press

Bake at 350 degrees F for approx 15 mins

Tops crack when done

Cool on wire rack

Ivy Bishop's Melt-in-the-Mouth Gingerbread

Ingredients

- 25 g butter, cubed
- ½ cup caster sugar
- ½ tsp ground ginger
- 2 ½ tsp ground cinnamon
- ¼ cup sweetened condensed milk
- 1 egg
- 2 ½ cups plain flour
- 1 tsp baking powder

Directions

1. Preheat oven to moderate heat.
2. Line two trays with baking paper.
3. Beat butter and sugar until light and creamy. Mix in ginger and cinnamon, sweetened condensed milk and egg.
4. Add sifted flour and baking powder. Mold mixture into a ball, wrap in cling film and refrigerate 10-15 minutes.
5. Cut dough in half. Roll out between sheets of baking paper or on floured bench. Cut out gingerbread men or other Christmas shapes. Repeat with rest of dough.
6. Bake until golden. Cool and decorate but most of all enjoy.

Happy Christmas :)

ABOUT THE AUTHORS AND CREATION OF MARIETTA

Anatomy of a Multi-Author Series

by Lilian Darcy

When I told ARRA's Debbie Phillips about the launch of a new mini-series from a new imprint, Montana Born Books, by new boutique publisher Tule Publishing Group, she pricked up her ears. Could I possibly write an article charting the milestones in the process of bringing all this newness from its bud-like idea stage to its full-blown rose of publishing glory? (Okay, she may not have put it quite like this. But she did use the word 'milestones'.)

Since it's been an enormously fun and satisfying year of milestone passing, I happily accepted the assignment.

It began in February ...

Milestone #1—The phone call

Jane Porter calls me from California. Jane is a good friend, so I'm smiling when I hear her voice. 'I want to launch a publishing company', she says. 'Are you in?'

I think I'm *in* before she even gets to the word. We talk on the phone until my ear turns blue and I have to seek medical attention. The plan is ambitious. This will be a real publishing company, not simply a group of like-minded authors publishing independently with some linked stories and branding (although, hey, that would be great, too). We will bring in experienced professionals in publishing, editing and marketing, as well as authors whose attitude and quality of work we can count on.

Honestly, I think my whole world feels different after this one phone call.

Milestone #2—The preparation

'I want you to come over here,' Jane says in a follow-up email. 'I have Megan Crane and CJ Carmichael on board, and we all need to get together to talk about our story ideas, and about how this is going to work.'

Did I mention that Jane is a good friend? She has frequent flyer miles that she actually *gives* me to cover the airline ticket. We decide May will be the best time, so I naturally go straight to the most vital pieces of preparation— crossing the days off a calendar and shopping for clothes.

We do also brainstorm a lot via email about stories during these two months. We decide to create the Montana Born Books imprint, and to set our first few series of books in our fictional town of Marietta, Montana. (Because

Montana is cool. I've been there now, and I know.)

We each throw in a bunch of ideas. Megan comes up with a big, single title mini-series about three sisters who've grown up with the difficult parenting of their saloon-owner and Vietnam vet father, Jason Grey, after their mother left town. CJ creates a traditional ranching family, the Carrigans, while Jane also creates a ranching family, the Sheenans, on the adjacent property. I have a major women's fiction trilogy in mind, following the lives of characters who've all been changed by what happened at the Marietta High School Prom in 1996.

Milestone #3—The brainstorming

May 1st arrives, and I fly across the Pacific to California. Jane meets me at LAX and nearly drives off the road about nine times on the way down to her house in San Clemente because we're so busy talking. Three days later, we fly to Kalispell, Montana, where CJ picks us up, after collecting Megan earlier in the day, and we drive to her cottage on Flathead Lake.

Now, some of you may have seen the pictures on Facebook, but I want to stress that we actually do work quite hard, despite appearances to the contrary.

First, we talk for a whole day, building our fictional universe. Where exactly is our town located? What's the population? What's its history? What stores and other buildings are there in Main Street? Who owns them? (Hint: When you read the books, watch out for mentions of a Jane Austen–inspired character, who's a bit of a gossip-monger.)

We go to bed very satisfied with our first day's work, and then the next morning when we get up CJ says, 'You know what? I don't think our planned stories are closely enough linked.'

She's right, we realize at once. We've each gone off on our own tangent, with the Carrigans, the Greys, the Sheenans and my tragic 1996 prom night. For our launch, we need something that knits our characters more closely together and celebrates our fictional town in a more vibrant way.

Milestone #4—The stories

'How about a rodeo?' I think this is CJ, too. She is so great at cutting to the heart of the problem and coming up with the right idea.

'Full-length stories?'

'No, how about a novella each?'

As writers, you tend to know something is right when the sparks immediately catch fire. Within an hour, this morning, we've each come up with the basic bones for a story. The Title Fairy pays us a visit, which is close to being a Montana Miracle. She is a pretty temperamental creature, that one, and can withhold her creativity for months, sometimes.

Armed with titles, story ideas, linking threads and a whole lot of detail on our fictional world, some of us begin writing this very day ...

This article first appeared in the September 2013 issue of the Australian Romance Readers Association newsletter. Reproduced with permission.

Founding Authors

Jane Porter

New York Times and USA Today bestselling author of forty-nine romances and women's fiction titles, Jane Porter has been a finalist for the prestigious RITA award five times and won in 2014 for Best Novella with her story, Take Me, Cowboy, from Tule Publishing. Today, Jane has over 12 million copies in print, including her wildly successful, Flirting With Forty, picked by Redbook as its Red Hot Summer Read, and reprinted six times in seven weeks before being made into a Lifetime movie starring Heather Locklear. A mother of three sons, Jane holds an MA in Writing from the University of San Francisco and makes her home in sunny San Clemente, CA with her surfer husband and two dogs.

Visit Jane's website at JanePorter.com

CJ Carmichael

USA Today bestselling author C. J. Carmichael has written over 45 novels in her favorite genres of romance and mystery. She has been nominated twice for the *Romance Writers of America* RITA Award, as well as *RT Bookclub's* Career Achievement in Romantic Suspense award, and the *Bookseller's Best* honor.

She gave up the thrills of income tax forms and double entry book-keeping in 1998 when she sold her first book to Harlequin Superromance. Since then she has published over 35 novels with Harlequin and is currently working on a series of Western romances with Tule Publishing. In addition C. J. Carmichael has published several cozy mystery series as an indie author.

When not writing C. J. enjoys family time with her grown daughters and her husband. Family dinners are great. Even better are the times they spend hiking in the Rocky Mountains around their home in Calgary, and relaxing at their cottage on Flathead Lake, Montana.

Visit C.J.'s website at CJCarmichael.com

Megan Crane

USA Today bestselling, RITA-nominated, and critically-acclaimed author Megan Crane has written more than sixty books since her debut in 2004. She has been published by a variety of publishers, including each of New York's Big Five. She's won fans with her women's fiction, chick lit, and work-for-hire young adult novels as well as with the Harlequin Presents she writes as Caitlin Crews. These days her focus is on contemporary romance from small town to international glamor, cowboys to bikers, and beyond. She sometimes teaches creative writing classes both online at mediabistro.com and at UCLA Extension's prestigious Writers' Program, where she finally utilizes the MA and PhD in English Literature she received from the University of York in York, England. She currently lives in the Pacific Northwest with a husband who draws comics and animation storyboards and their menagerie of ridiculous animals.

Visit Megan's website at MeganCrane.com

Lilian Darcy

Lilian Darcy was born on Valentine's Day. This auspicious date, as well as a love of reading, set her destiny as a writer of romance and women's fiction from an early age. She has also written extensively for Australian theater and television, under another name. Her plays have been professionally performed by some of Australia's most prestigious theater companies, and have received two award nominations for Best Play from the Australian Writers Guild, while in 1990 she was the co-recipient of an Australian Film Institute award for best TV mini-series. She has now written over eighty romances for Harlequin, as well as several mainstream novels, including Cafe du Jour, originally published by Mira Books Australia.

Montana Born Authors

Barbara Ankrum

Barbara Ankrum has a thing for the West and has written both historical and contemporary romances, all set in that magical place. Twice nominated for RWA's RITA Award, her bestselling books are emotional, sexy rides with a touch of humor. Barbara's married and raised two children in Southern California, which, in her mind, makes her a native Westerner.

Visit Barbara's website at BarbaraAnkrum.com

Robin Bielman

When not attached to her laptop, USA Today bestselling author and RITA Finalist, Robin Bielman loves to read, take hikes with her hubby, and frequent coffee shops. A California girl, the beach is her favorite place for fun, relaxation, and inspiration.

She loves to go on adventures, and has skydived, scuba dived, parasailed, gotten lost in the wilderness (and only suffered a gazillion bug bites for it) hiked to waterfalls, and swam with dolphins. In her spare time she also tries to put her treadmill to good use while watching her favorite TV shows, indulges her sweet tooth, and plays a mean game of sock tug of war with her cute, but sometimes naughty dog, Harry.

Writing is a dream come true, and she still pinches herself to be sure it's real. She lives in Southern California with her high school sweetheart husband and loves to connect with readers. Get the scoop on Robin, her books, and sign up for her newsletter on her website.

Visit Robin's website at RobinBielman.com

Kim Boykin

Kim Boykin is a women's fiction author with a sassy Southern streak. She is the author of *The Wisdom of Hair*, *Steal Me* and *Palmetto Moon*. While her heart is always in South Carolina, she lives in Charlotte, North Carolina, with her husband, three dogs, and 126 rose bushes.

Visit Kim's website at KimBoykin.com

Alissa Callen

When not writing Alissa Callen plays traffic controller to four children, three dogs, two horses and one renegade cow who really does believe the grass is greener on the other side of the fence. After a childhood spent chasing sheep on the family farm, she has always been drawn to remote areas and small towns, even when residing overseas. Once a teacher and a counselor, she remains interested in the life journeys people take. Her books are characteristically heart-warming, emotional and character driven. She currently lives on a small slice of rural Australia.

Visit Alissa's website at AlissaCallen.com

Dani Collins

Award winning and USA Today bestselling author, Dani Collins, has written more than two dozen romances ranging from sexy contemporary for Harlequin Presents, to romantic comedy, epic medieval fantasy and even some erotic romance. Lately she has also been writing rancher romance for Tule's Montana Born. Since she's a small town girl at heart, this makes her feel at home.

Dani lives in Canada with her high school sweetheart and two mostly-grown children.

Visit Dani's website at DaniCollins.com

Eve Gaddy

Eve Gaddy is the best-selling award-winning author of more than seventeen novels. Her books have won and been nominated for awards from Romantic Times, Golden Quill, Bookseller's Best, Holt Medallion, Texas Gold, Daphne Du Maurier and more. She was nominated for a Romantic Times Career Achievement Award for Innovative Series romance as well as winning the 2008 Romantic Times Career Achievement award for Series Storyteller of the year. Eve's books have sold over a million copies worldwide and been published in many foreign countries. Eve lives in East Texas with her husband of many years.

Visit Eve's website at EveGaddy.net

Katherine Garbera

USA Today bestselling author Katherine Garbera is a two-time Maggie winner who has written more than 60 books. A Florida native who grew up to travel the globe, Katherine now makes her home in the Midlands of the UK with her husband, two children and a very spoiled miniature dachshund.

Visit Katherine's website at KatherineGarbera.com

Kate Hardy

Kate Hardy is the award-winning author of more than 60 novels for Harlequin, Entangled and Tule Publishing.

She lives in Norwich in the east of England with her husband, two teenage children, a springer spaniel called Byron, and too many books to count. She's a bit of a science and history nerd who loves cinema, the theater, and baking (which is why you'll find her in the gym five mornings a week – oh, and to ballroom dancing lessons). She loves doing research, especially if it means something hands-on and exploring. That's how the ballroom dancing started…

Visit Kate's website at KateHardy.com

Nicole Helm

Nicole Helm writes down-to-earth contemporary romance—from farmers to cowboys, Midwest to *the* west, she writes stories about people finding themselves and finding love in the process. She lives in Missouri with her husband and two sons, surrounded by light sabers, video games, and a shared dream of someday owning a farm.

Visit Nicole's website at NicoleHelm.wordpress.com

Kelly Hunter

Accidentally educated in the sciences, Kelly Hunter didn't think to start writing romances until she was surrounded by the jungles of Malaysia for a year and didn't have anything to read. Eventually she decided that writing romance suited her far better than throwing sterile screw-worm flies out of airplane windows, and changed careers. Kelly now lives in Australia, surrounded by lush farmland and family, 2 dogs, 3 miniature cows, a miniature pig, a 3-legged cat and a small flock of curious chickens. There are still flies, but their maggots don't feed on flesh. Bargain. Kelly is a USA Today bestselling author, a three-time Romance Writers of America RITA finalist and loves writing to the short contemporary romance form.

Visit Kelly's website at KellyHunter.net

Sinclair Jayne

Sinclair has loved reading romance novels since she discovered Barbara Cartland historical romances when she was in sixth grade. By seventh grade, she was haunting the library shelves looking to fall in love over and over again with the heroes born from the imaginations of her favorite authors. After teaching writing classes and workshops to adults and teens for many years in Seattle and Portland, she returned to her first love of reading romances and became an editor for Tule Publishing last year. Sinclair lives in Oregon's wine country where she and her family own a small vineyard of Pinot Noir and where she dreams of being able to write at a desk like Jane Austen instead of in parking lots waiting for her kids to finish one of their 12,000 extracurricular activities.

Visit Sinclair's website at SinclairJayne.com

Rachael Johns

Rachael Johns is an English teacher by trade, a mum 24/7, a supermarket owner, a chronic arachnophobe, and a writer the rest of the time. She rarely sleeps and never irons. She writes contemporary romance and lives in rural Western Australia with her hyperactive husband, three mostly-gorgeous heroes-in-training, two fat cats, a cantankerous bird and a very naughty dog. Rachael loves to hear from readers.

Visit Rachael's website at RachaelJohns.com

Kat Latham

Kat Latham writes sexy contemporary romance, including the London Legends rugby series.

She's a California girl who moved to Europe the day after graduating from UCLA, ditching her tank tops for raincoats. She spent several years teaching English in Prague followed by several more working for a humanitarian organization in London. She now lives with her British husband and baby girl in a small town in the rural Netherlands surrounded by miles and miles of green pasture, canals and Shetland ponies. Kat's slowly adjusting to life in a place where bicycles and cows seem to outnumber people.

When she's not traveling, reading or writing, Kat can be found sharing overly personal things on her blog, Twitter and Facebook.

Visit Kat's website at KatLatham.com

Yvonne Lindsay

A typical Piscean, USA Today bestselling author, Yvonne Lindsay, has always preferred the stories in her head to the real world. It makes perfect sense that she was born and bred in Middle Earth, um, New Zealand. Yvonne has published over twenty-five titles with Harlequin and is a three-time Romance Writers of Australia R*BY nominee. A former law office manager, she now spends her days crafting the stories of her heart and in her spare time she can be found with her nose firmly in a book, reliving the power of love in all walks of life, or knitting socks and daydreaming.

Visit Yvonne's website at YvonneLindsay.com

Sarah Mayberry

Sarah Mayberry is the award-winning, bestselling author of more than 30 novels. She was born in Melbourne, Australia, and is the middle of three children. Sarah picked up a love of romance novels from both her grandmothers and has always wanted to be a writer. In line with this ambition, she completed a Bachelor of Arts degree in Professional Writing and Literature. It took her ten years and multiple attempts before her first book was accepted. During that time, Sarah worked in magazine publishing and the television industry, contributing to the internationally known Australian serial drama "Neighbours" and co-creating teen drama series "Karaoke High". Sarah currently splits her time between writing for television and writing novels. She lives in Melbourne by the bay with her husband and a small, furry Cavoodle called Max. When she isn't writing, she loves reading, cooking, going to the movies and buying shoes.

Visit Sarah's website at SarahMayberry.com

Anne McAllister

Best-selling author Anne McAllister has written nearly 70 romance novels—long and short, contemporary, time travel, and single title. She has won two RITA awards from the Romance Writers of America and has had nine other books which were RITA finalists. Anne grew up on the beaches of Southern California, and spent summers in Montana and on her grandparents' small ranch in Colorado. They were formative experiences—not only in providing her settings, but in giving her heroes. She finds herself attracted to lean, dark, honorable men – often lone wolf types – who always get the job done, whatever it might be. After spending two-thirds of her life near the Mississippi River in Iowa, Anne and her husband, The Prof, now live in Montana with two dogs—right down the road from her four youngest grandkids who are intent on keeping her busy. But no matter how busy she is, Anne will always be writing. She has too many ideas not to!

Visit Anne's website at AnneMcAllister.com

Melissa McClone

Melissa McClone's degree in mechanical engineering from Stanford University led her to a job with a major airline where she travelled the globe and met her husband. But analyzing jet engine performance couldn't compete with her love of writing happily ever afters. Her first full-time writing endeavor was her first sale when she was pregnant with her first child! Since then, she has published over twenty-five romance novels with Harlequin and been nominated for Romance Writers of America's RITA award. When she isn't writing, she's usually driving her minivan to/from her children's swim and soccer practices, 4-H meetings and dog shows. She also supports deployed service members through Soldiers' Angels and fosters cats through a local non-kill rescue shelter. Melissa lives in the Pacific Northwest with her husband, three school-aged children, two spoiled Norwegian elkhounds and cats who think they rule the house.

Visit Melissa's website at MelissaMcClone.com

Jeannie Moon

Jeannie Moon has always been a romantic. When she's not spinning tales of her own, Jeannie works as a school librarian, thankful she has a job that allows her to immerse herself in books and call it work. Married to her high school sweetheart, Jeannie has three kids, three lovable dogs and a mischievous cat and lives in her hometown on Long Island, NY. If she's more than ten miles away from salt water for any longer than a week, she gets twitchy.

Visit Jeannie's website at JeannieMoon.com

Trish Morey

USA Today bestselling author, Trish Morey has written thirty romances for the internationally bestselling Harlequin Presents line and her stories have been published in more than 25 languages in 40 countries worldwide, including being published in manga comic book form in Japan, and as Trish Moreyova in the Czech Republic. Trish was awarded Romance Writers of Australia's Romantic Book of the Year Award (the Ruby) for short, sexy romance in 2006 and again in 2009, as well as being a finalist in the Romance Writers of America's prestigious RITA Awards in 2012. A qualified chartered accountant by trade, Trish was employed as financial manager at a major business school prior to her first sale. Trish lives with her husband, 4 daughters and assorted menagerie in the beautiful Adelaide Hills.

Visit Trish's website at TrishMorey.com

Kathleen O'Brien

 After a short career as a feature writer and TV critic, Kathleen O'Brien turned to writing romance, and the job fit so well she never looked back. Now she's published more than forty titles, is a five-time finalist for the Romance Writers of America's RITA award, and holds an MFA in Writing Popular Fiction from Seton Hill University. She lives near Orlando with her former-journalist husband, just down the road from their two grown children and, of course, the ever-famous Mouse.

Visit Kathleen's website at KObrienonline.com

Terri Reed

Award winning multi-published author Terri Reed discovered the wonderful world of fiction at an early age and declared she would one day write a book. Now she is fulfilling that dream writing full-time. Her romance and romantic suspense novels have appeared on Publisher's Weekly top 25, Nielsen's Bookscan top 100 and featured in USA Today, Christian Fiction Magazine and Romantic Times Magazine. Her books have finaled in Romance Writers of America's RITA contest, National Reader's Choice Award contest and three times in American Christian Fiction Writers The Carol Award contest. She resides in the Pacific Northwest with her college-sweetheart husband, two wonderful children, and an array of critters. When not writing, she enjoys spending time with her family and friends, gardening and playing tennis.

Visit Terri's website at TerriReed.com

Nancy Robards Thompson

Award-winning author Nancy Robards Thompson has worked as a newspaper reporter, television show stand-in, production and casting assistant for movies, and in fashion and public relations. She started writing fiction seriously in 1997. Five years and four completed manuscripts later, she won the Romance Writers of America's Golden Heart award for unpublished writers and sold her first book the following year. Since then, Nancy has sold 30 books and found her calling doing what she loves most – writing romance and women's fiction full-time.

Visit Nancy's website at NancyRobardsThompson.com

Debra Salonen

Former award-winning newspaper journalist Debra Salonen is a nationally bestselling author with 26 published novels for Harlequin's Superromance and American lines and one single title release for Harlequin Signature. Several of her titles were nominated for "Best Superromance," including UNTIL HE MET RACHEL, which took home that honor in 2010. Debra was named Romantic Times Reviewer's Career Achievement "Series Storyteller of the Year" in 2006. Debra lives in the foothills near Yosemite National Park in California with her husband and two dogs. Luckily, her two children and three grandchildren live close by to keep Debra connected to the real world.

Visit Debra's website at DebraSalonen.com

Charlene Sands

Charlene Sands is a USA Today bestselling author writing sexy contemporary romances and stories set in the Old West. Her stories have been honored with the National Readers Choice Award, the Cataromance Reviewer's Choice Award and she's a double recipient of the Booksellers' Best Award. She was recently honored with Romantic Times Magazine's Best Harlequin Desire of 2014. Charlene is a member of the Orange County Chapter and Los Angeles Chapter of Romance Writers of America.

When not writing, she enjoys great coffee, spending time with her four "princesses," bowling in a women's league, country music, reading books from her favorite authors and going on movie dates with her "hero" husband. Sign up for her newsletter at www.charlenesands.com for new releases and special member giveaways. Charlene loves hearing from her readers on Facebook, Twitter and Instagram.

Bold, strong, heart-melting heroes… and always real good men.

Visit Charlene's website at CharleneSands.com

Roxanne Snopek

Born under a Scorpio moon, raised in a little house on the prairie, USA Today bestselling author Roxanne Snopek said "as you wish" to her alpha farm boy and followed him to the mountain air and ocean breezes of British Columbia. There, while healing creatures great and small and raising three warrior-princesses, they found their real-life happily-ever-after. After also establishing a successful freelance and non-fiction career, Roxanne began writing what she most loved to read: romance. Her small-town stories quickly became fan favorites for their humor and heart-tugging emotion. She has two titles appearing in the upcoming The Chocolate Shop Books series, three full-length novels in a new print series called Sunset Bay launching in 2017, and no plans to slow down.

Visit Roxanne's website at RoxanneSnopek.ca

Joanne Walsh

Joanne Walsh became hooked on romance when her grandma gave her a copy of Gone with the Wind for her birthday. The teachers at her strict girls' school didn't approve of a ten-year-old reading such a 'racy' novel and confiscated it. But Joanne still became a voracious romance reader and, later, an editor for one of the world's leading women's fiction publishers, where she could do two of her favorite things: work with her beloved alpha-male heroes and spend time in the USA. These days, Joanne lives in the south of England and divides her time between freelance editing, writing and spending time with her very own real-life alpha...

Scarlet Wilson

Scarlet Wilson wrote her first story at age 8 and has never stopped. She's worked in the health service for over 20 years, training as a nurse and a health visitor, and now currently works within public health. Writing romances is a dream come true for Scarlet and she's published with Harlequin Mills and Boon, Tule Publishing and Entangled Publishing. Scarlet lives on the West Coast of Scotland with her fiancé and their two sons. She loves to hear from readers and can be reached via her website.

Visit Scarlet's website at Scarlet-Wilson.com

Maisey Yates

USA Today bestselling author Maisey Yates lives in rural Oregon with her three children and her husband, whose chiseled jaw and arresting features continue to make her swoon. She feels the epic trek she takes several times a day from her office to her coffee maker is a true example of her pioneer spirit.

In 2009, at the age of twenty-three Maisey sold her first book. Since then it's been a whirlwind of sexy alpha males and happily ever afters, and she wouldn't have it any other way. Maisey divides her writing time between dark, passionate category romances set just about everywhere on earth and light sexy contemporary romances set practically in her back yard. She believes that she clearly has the best job in the world.

Visit Maisey's website at MaiseyYates.com

Thank you for reading the Book Girl's Guide to Marietta.

To keep up with the latest Marietta releases, visit
www.tulepublishing.com.

To hang out with your favorite Montana Born authors and
readers who love Marietta as much as you do,
join Main St. Marietta on Facebook,
an exclusive group for lovers of
contemporary Western romance.

TULE
PUBLISHING